995259

When all else fails...

read the directions

Bob Smith

Considering God's Plan for a Living Church

When all
else fails...

read the
directions

Foreword by HOWARD G. HENDRICKS

WORD BOOKS
PUBLISHER
Waco, Texas

Scripture quotations, unless otherwise marked
are from The Revised Standard Version of the Bible,
copyright 1946 (renewed 1973), 1956 and © 1971
by the Division of Christian Education of the
National Council of the Churches of Christ in
the United States of America, and are used
by permission.

Scripture quotations marked NAS are from
The New American Standard Bible © The Lockman
Foundation 1960, 1962, 1963, 1968, 1971.

ISBN 0-87680-985-9

Library of Congress catalog card number: 74-77615
Printed in the United States of America

First Printing—July 1974
First Paperback Printing—May 1975
Second Paperback Printing—May 1976
Third Paperback Printing, June 1977
Fourth Paperback Printing, July 1978

Illustrations by Vic Persson
Cover design by David Smith

DEDICATION

I'd like to dedicate this book to the two whose love makes life so great for me: the Lord Jesus, who knows all about me and loves me anyway; and my darling wife, Pearl, who knows more about me than anyone and still loves me—with the same faithfulness and constancy of commitment as the Lord himself.

My fervent hope is that my response to both the Lord and Pearl will contribute to the fulfillment of their own hearts' desire.

ACKNOWLEDGEMENTS

I am deeply indebted to my fellow pastors and workers in the church we jointly serve, for all I have learned through them of the truth of God both by what they teach and how they walk. I am no less grateful to a wonderfully open-hearted board of elders, whose response of faith to the directives of the great Head of the church, the Lord Jesus Christ, has made possible the recording of his activities in our midst.

Special thanks are due my dear friend, Dr. Donald Rhodes, whose encouragement moved me to action.

Knowing something of the heartbeat of all these, I'm sure they would join me in dedicating this effort to all the dear people of God who comprise the church, and to the One whose heart longs for the complete fulfillment and enjoyment of all he bought and paid for in his redeeming grace.

For God ". . . has made him head over all things for the church, which is his body, the fulness of him who fills all in all" (Eph. 1:22–23).

CONTENTS

               A collection of practical materials for use in
               equipping the saints: outlines, sample study
               sheets, suggestions for further study, and
               questions with answers—all related to the
               Scriptures and the text of the book

FOREWORD

Every generation must wage its own unique theological battles. The sediment in the muddy waters of the 1970s settles into the issues of the doctrine of the church. Men and women—young people in particular—are spitting out the tasteless, lukewarm experience of the church to which they have been exposed. But the question nags, are they rejecting the church as designed by Christ or are they repudiating the church as denigrated by men? Perhaps we have offered them a caricature of the real thing. They may be rejecting the wrong item.

Resurrection is difficult in any realm. But Pastor Robert Smith dares to believe that these bones can live again when infused with the power and life of the risen Head of the church, Jesus Christ.

Bob Smith is no armchair theorist. He has been in the ball game. Since its inception, I have been privileged to see Peninsula Bible Church and this committed servant up close. I have watched him in the superb teamwork of that fellowship hammer out his concepts on the anvil of personal involvement. His concepts have been tested in the laboratory of reality experience.

Few men have earned the high respect of his peers and colleagues as has Robert Smith. He is a producer and above all a man of God. With clarity and simplicity, true to his personality, he has answered the who-when-what-why-where of his subject. Further, with his characteristic light touch, he has spelled out the all-important *how* in realistic, contemporary, but intensely biblical terms.

11

The book is neither pedantic nor blandly academic. Rather, it moves with informational and motivational dynamic. It will provoke a hundred questions in the reader's mind. In the final analysis, the test of a book like this is not what it does for you, but what you do with it.

One of the highest peaks is the final chapter where letters are addressed to twentieth century churches, such as the "Church at Bible City" and "The First Right Wing Church." Here remarkably penetrating and incisive questions are posed. The reader cannot pass by without thinking—long and hard.

It has been my high privilege to know Bob Smith personally for many years, and I commend his writing to you. I have long been impatient for him to express his excellent ideas in print. His hesitancy has been admirable, because he did not want to shoot from the lip. With nourishing experience behind him, he has now ministered significantly to the Body by sharing what God has shared with him. We are all the beneficiaries.

Howard G. Hendricks
Professor of Christian Education
Dallas Theological Seminary

PREFACE

There is dynamic and exciting action in the new breed of young Christians. When I contrast their contagious enthusiasm with the dull and dispirited state of the church in general, my heart says there ought to be a better way than we've been going. And when I add to that the sad picture of the Lord Jesus being robbed of his inheritance in the saints I sense *someone* ought to be speaking out loud and clear on the church in terms of our Lord's operational scheme—the biblical pattern. Somehow the Lord got the message across to me, "How about you?" So here goes!

You may find areas of disagreement with my statements, and that is certainly your privilege—but please be open to consider whether you are arguing with me or with the Lord, will you? For I have made every effort to convey only what is sustainable on biblical grounds and demonstrable in practical experience; otherwise I'm convinced this book would have no real value. I have no motive other than to contribute to the strengthening and building of Christ's church.

I am not so naive as to think I have the last word on how the church should function, but neither do I think that most of us have even begun to understand and operate on the basis of the biblical information. My hope is to be able to alert all of us to the need for reexamining *what the Lord has to say to the church* so that somehow between us we can complete the picture drawn in vivid detail in the New Testament. You can write the sequel— let us hope in the form of living letters spelled out in live churches,

13

where the Lord of the church is enjoying the full use of his Living Body.

Right now I see an arthritic church, with joints all swollen and deformed, causing the Body (including the Head) to hurt.

Would you seek with me a cure for this debilitating and painful disease?

Bob Smith

WHEN ALL ELSE FAILS...

CHAPTER ONE

CAN IT BE?

". . . I will build my church; and the gates of hell shall not prevail against it."—Matthew 16:18b, AV

These are the words of Jesus Christ—a confident declaration that, as unlikely as it seems, his church is winning, not losing, in the battle against unseen demonic powers. And the apostle Paul confirms when he writes: ". . . Christ loved the church and gave himself up for her . . . that he might present the church to himself in splendor, without spot or wrinkle or any such thing, that she might be holy and without blemish" (Eph. 5:25–27).

We see how badly the church has missed the mark and we must

15

admit it seems highly unlikely our Lord can make good on these statements. We look at ourselves as Christians and see that we ourselves have a long way to go "to be conformed to the image of God's Son" (Rom. 8:29). Can he do it?

The world looks at the church with utter disdain. They're betting their life Jesus is a dreamer—and that we'll never make it. But I, for one, am fully persuaded our Lord will accomplish all that he said in regard to his church. Not one word of his claims can be denied! His predictions, his ministry of compassion, his miracles, his victory over death, his matchless character all shout out loud that he tells the truth because he *is* the truth. Even skeptics don't consider him a liar! Deluded, maybe—or naive about the facts of life (as we now know them in this enlightened scientific age) perhaps—but not a deliberate liar. His life and ministry in fulfillment of his claims do not leave us this option.

So, I have no doubt. He's going to make it—and so are we, I do believe!

A Credibility Gap

But why is there such a wide discrepancy between our Lord's triumphant declaration and the sad state of the church? That's the pointed question we need to face. The answer seems readily apparent: we are just not cooperating with his program. We keep wanting to do it *our* way, and he keeps insisting, "Be reasonable, do it *my* way!" Have you ever tried to assemble a knocked-down bicycle, or puzzle, or appliance? I'll lay odds—if you're like me— you have tried to do it on your own, made a mess of it and finally said to yourself, "When all else fails, read the directions!"

The appeal of this book is to encourage all of us to *read the directions.* They have been on record in the New Testament for centuries. Will you review with me the way Christ has designed to build his church?

Be careful! It might mean some radical changes in your thinking!

High Stakes

The stakes are high for every Christian in this matter, for there is coming a day of evaluation for all of us. It's strange how many

Christians seem to think that because salvation is by grace, what we do with our lives as Christians doesn't really matter. Nothing could be farther from the truth if we believe God's Word on this subject: "For we must all be brought to the light in front of the tribunal of Christ, that each one may receive what he practiced through the body, whether *good* or *worthless*" (2 Cor. 5:10, a literal rendering).

Note that the Scripture does not say whether *good* or *evil* but whether good or *worthless*. It is not sin that is in view here; it is value that will count in our Lord's final consideration of our earthly life and ministry.

The Bible is very clear that there are rewards to be gained—or lost.

> For no other foundation can any one lay than that which is laid, which is Jesus Christ. Now if any one builds on the foundation with gold, silver, precious stones, wood, hay, stubble—each man's work will become manifest; for the Day will disclose it, because it will be revealed with fire, and the fire will test what sort of work each one has done. If the work which any man has built on the foundation survives, he will receive a reward. If any man's work is burned up, he will suffer loss, though he himself will be saved, but only as through fire (1 Cor. 3:11–15).

Builders or wreckers?

Note here the foundation on which we build is a *person*—Jesus Christ our Lord. But what are the exotic building materials? I've never seen a house built of gold or silver. Stones, yes, but not precious stones! So obviously this is figurative language. But what do the figures represent?

First, it seems clear that there are two distinctive kinds of material: those that burn and those that don't. Since they are to be tried by fire, it's important to build with fireproof materials. Here fire pictures the judgment of God, consuming everything that does not have lasting, eternal value. But is there further meaning in "gold, silver and precious stones"? If we believe in an inspired text there must be a reason these words were chosen. After all, the writer could have said something else, like "brick and mortar." So, we look for some deeper significance. Here's what I discovered as I thought it through.

Gold in the Bible, when used in a figurative sense, represents deity or divine activity. Remember the Ark of the Covenant in Exodus? It was acacia wood overlaid, inside and out, with gold. The ark represented the presence of God among men and was the "meeting place" where God and man could meet. Thus it pictures the incarnate Christ: the wood, his humanity and gold, his deity. Regarding our works, then, *God must be in them* for them to have eternal, abiding value.

How about the *silver?* Again, looking to the Old Testament, we see that silver represents redemption. The redemption coin, the shekel, was a silver coin. From this we understand that our works must be redemptive to have any value before God, because he is a redemptive God!

The *precious stones*—what are they? Well, this is not hard to discover. Peter says, "Come to him, to that living stone, rejected by men but in God's sight chosen and precious; and like living stones be yourselves built into a spiritual house, to be a holy priesthood, to offer spiritual sacrifices acceptable to God through Jesus Christ" (1 Pet. 2:4-5). The precious (or *costly*) stones are clearly living believers, built into a holy temple where God is resident in his people.

Thus it appears the criteria for enduring works are established here. For our work to have eternal value:

- •It must be built on the proper foundation, Jesus Christ.
- •God must be in it.
- •It must be redemptive.
- •It must involve people being rightly related to God as his dwelling place.

Consider Jesus

High stakes for us, yes—but also for our Lord. He would like to have the full use of his Body. Changing the figure, he would also enjoy the full habitation of his royal residence. This is why our Lord Jesus expressed the desire of his heart so fervently to the Father in prayer:

As thou didst send me into the world, so I have sent them into the world. And for their sake I consecrate myself, that they also may be consecrated in truth. I do not pray for these only, but also for those who believe in me through their word, *that they may all be one;* even as thou, Father, art in me, and I in thee, that they also may be in us, so that the world may believe that thou hast sent me. The glory which thou hast given me I have given to them, *that they may be one even as we are one,* I in them and thou in me, *that they may become perfectly one,* so that the world may know that thou hast sent me and hast loved them even as thou hast loved me. Father, I desire that they also, whom thou hast given me, may be with me where I am, to behold my glory which thou hast given me in thy love for me before the foundation of the world. O righteous Father, *the world has not known thee,* but I have known thee; and these know that thou hast sent me. I made known to them thy name, and I will make it known, *that the love with which thou hast loved me may be in them, and I in them* (John 17:18–26).

His emphasis here is so obviously our *oneness* in the Body of Christ, and the expression of his life and love to a world that doesn't know him—*through that Body.*

So how is it with us? Are we cooperating with Christ in building his church? Are we following his plan? That which we're doing right now—is it good or worthless in the appraising eye of the One who has a right to expect results? After all, he paid a high price to redeem us. Are we giving him all he bought and paid for at such great cost to himself?

And how is your church doing? Is it dead or alive?

If it could use a new birth of freedom, read on! Let's find out where we missed the way and go back to doing it by the Book.

"You are not your own; you were bought with a price."
—1 Corinthians 6:20

WHO'S RUNNING THE SHOW?

CHAPTER TWO

THE LIVING CHURCH

The church as described in the New Testament is very much alive. It is described as a *living organism,* designed to operate very much like the human body with its intricate interrelationship of many parts and functions. This figure is employed particularly in Paul's New Testament letters about the church, as in Ephesians 4:15–16: ". . . we are to grow up in every way into him who is the head, into Christ, from whom *the whole body, joined and knit together by every joint with which it is supplied,* when each part is working properly, makes bodily growth and upbuilds itself in love."

We'd like to focus our attention on the phrase, "every joint with which it is supplied." For just as in the human body, the church which is the Body of Christ must have joints and tendons and sinews which hold it together and enable it to function as a coordinated whole. In a local church the joints and sinews are the administrative links which enable everything to hang together and operate smoothly, and without which the church functions poorly and ineffectively.

Who's Running the Show?

Twentieth-century church life and government are often characterized by one of two patterns: (1) the church is "run" by a dominant personality, usually the pastor, but sometimes even by a dominant female figure in the congregation, or (2) it is governed by democratic procedures. Neither of these even approximates the biblical plan of church government.

Just ask me—I'll tell you what to do

The "dominant figure" brand of church government is mentioned in the New Testament only in negative terms. In one instance, Diotrephes is cited as one "who likes to put himself first" (3 John 9). In another, the Nicolaitans, in teaching and deeds, are clearly rebuked by the Lord in Revelation 2:6 and 15. The only clue we have to their error is in the meaning of the name. "Nicolaitans" is a term derived from the Greek words nikao, "to conquer"; and laos, "people." It thus portrays the "dominant figure" type of church operation. This is a concept which incurs the strong censure of the Lord in his word: ". . . you hate the deeds of the Nicolaitans which I also hate" (Rev. 2:6), and ". . . you also have some who in the same way hold the teaching of the Nicolaitans. Repent therefore . . ." (Rev. 2:15–16).

The "dominant figure" approach is *not* God's way.

So . . . let's have an election

But nowhere in the New Testament is the church set forth as a democracy! To say in a democratic country that the church is not a democracy is like being against motherhood. But if we are really committed to the New Testament as our source book and standard, we need to face the problem squarely and check out the source information. Admittedly, it is hard for us to stop defending our own preconditioned ideas on this matter, but what is the final authority—the New Testament, or our personal preconceptions and ecclesiastical traditions?

Only one Head

To set the scene for understanding the biblical pattern, perhaps we should first recall that the Lord Jesus is presented in the New Testament as the Chief Shepherd (1 Pet. 5:4) and the Great Shepherd of the sheep (Heb. 13:20). So we need to ask the question, Who leads the flock, the shepherd or the sheep? The answer is readily apparent: no one ever expects a flock to lead its shepherd.

Then, too, Christ is set forth as the Head of the church which is his Body (Eph. 1:22–23). And it is obvious that orders proceed from the head to the body, not vice versa. It seems clear that the church is not to be a democracy, but a theocracy, with its rule coming from the Lord Jesus Christ, its exalted Head (Col. 1:18; 2:10, 18–19).

So much for theory

It seems, then, that a theory of church government is quite clearly spelled out in these concepts. But how is this worked out in practical detail? What human agency of governing authority has been stipulated in the New Testament? And could not the Head communicate directly to each member of his body and govern through democratic procedures?

To answer the last question first, there is no doubt that he could govern through a democratic structure, but that's not what he chose to do. Rather, he chose to say through his apostles, "Appoint elders in every town" (Tit. 1:5), and "Let the elders who rule well be considered worthy of double honor" (1 Tim. 5:17–22). Even as early in church history as Acts 20, Paul was able to call together the elders of the Ephesian church and charge them, "Take heed to yourselves and to all the flock in which the Holy Spirit has made you guardians, to feed the church of the Lord which he obtained with his own blood" (Acts 20:28).

Whose church is it?

Notice it is called "the church *of the Lord*," and the leaders are appointed as *"guardians*, to feed the church." Also, it was the Spirit of God who appointed them—not a democratic electoral process. Two words used in these verses describe those whom God made responsible for governing the church: *elders*, and *guardians*. The word *elder* speaks of maturity, in this case spiritual maturity —an obvious necessity for those who rule. And *guardians* are those charged with the responsibility of oversight, to see to the welfare of the flock and to care for the well-being of God's people.

In the book of Hebrews the writer says, "Remember your leaders who spoke to you the word of God . . ." (Heb. 13:7), and, "Obey your leaders and submit to them; for they are keeping watch over your souls as men who will have to give account. Let them do this joyfully and not sadly . . ." (Heb. 13:17).

Take me to your leaders

The biblical pattern of church government is laid out for us in terms of men who were called and appointed to the office of governing and leading the flock of God. But who appoints these elders or guardians? In actuality, the Holy Spirit does the appointing. He is the one who has given gifts for ministry— he knows who has the spiritual maturity and the leadership qualities which he himself imparts, thus he alone is qualified to make these appointments.

But, you say, this is still mysterious. What human agency does he use to let us know who it is he wants to lead and rule? Could he not still do this through a democratic election? We hasten to answer yes, he could. But what *did* he do? Let's check the record.

On the Care and Feeding of Sheep

The first appointment of an elder in the New Testament is reported in John 21 in the well-known scene between the Lord Jesus and the Apostle Peter. It reads like this:

> When they had finished breakfast, Jesus said to Simon Peter, "Simon, son of John, do you love me more than these?" He said to him, "Yes, Lord; you know that I love you." He said to him, *"Feed my lambs."* A second time he said to him, "Simon, son of John, do you love me?" He said to him, "Yes, Lord; you know that I love you." He said to him, *"Tend my sheep."* He said to him the third time, "Simon, son of John, do you love me?" Peter was grieved because he said to him the third time, "Do you love me?" And he said to him, "Lord, you know everything; you know that I love you." Jesus said to him, *"Feed my sheep"* (John 21:15–17).

We will not attempt a detailed study of this dialogue, but would like to highlight certain features that impinge on our present question. There are careful shades of meaning in this text.

Note that our Lord changed the wording each time he charged Peter. In John 21:15 he said, *"Feed* my lambs." In 21:16 he says, *"Tend* (literally, *shepherd*) my sheep." And in 21:17 he says, *"Feed* my sheep." It is significant to observe that the primary charge, that is, *"feed,"* is twice repeated, and in between the two he says, *"Shepherd* my sheep." The emphasis is clearly that feeding the flock is the main business of the elder but not the total of his responsibility; it is also his job to care *for* the sheep just as the Chief Shepherd himself does. The following chart may help to visualize this:

The Chief Shepherd appoints a pastor

(1) John 21:15	"feed"—involves expository teaching of God's Word. "As newborn babes desire [for them] the sincere milk of the word, that you may grow thereby" (1 Pet. 2:2, AV).	"my lambs"—has in mind the young believers [new Christians] as an object of primary concern.
(2) John 21:16	"shepherd"—includes training, discipling, counseling, comforting, encouraging, protecting, restoring, healing, etc.	"my sheep"—in the Greek a special qualified form expressing endearment, as "my dearly loved sheep."
(3) John 21:17	"feed"—same as (1) above, for "man shall not live by bread alone, but by every word that proceeds from the mouth of God" (Matt. 4:4 and Deut. 8:3).	"my sheep"—same as (2) above. Note: both times this includes all the flock, young and old alike, as distinct from (1) which has in view new believers in Christ.

Even Peter caught on

Here is a clear assignment of responsibility which Peter himself recognized as his, as seen in his first letter,

So I exhort the elders among you, as a fellow elder and a witness of the sufferings of Christ, as well as a partaker in the glory that is to be revealed. *Tend the flock of God that is in your charge* not by constraint but willingly, not for shameful gain but eagerly, not as domineering over those in your charge, but being examples to the flock. And when the Chief Shepherd is manifested you will obtain the unfading crown of glory (1 Pet. 5:1–4).

Note that the Scripture in 1 Peter 5 relates the terms *elder* and *shepherd* of the flock to the same person, in this case Peter himself. In John 21:16, *"shepherd* my sheep" is equivalent to Peter's appointment and assignment to be a pastor, or what we might call his ordination into a pastoral ministry. Peter's command to "tend the flock of God" (1 Pet. 5:2) is literally *"shepherd* the flock." From this idea we get the term *pastor.* A pastor is to be a *shepherd* of God's flock.

A job description—elder/guardian/pastor

To summarize, we have in the term *elder* the *basic qualification for leadership;* that is, spiritual maturity. In *guardian* we have set forth the *responsibility of oversight and accountability* to the Lord. And in the term *pastor* we have reflected *the heart attitude* necessary to fulfill the job. A pastor must be one who really has the care and feeding of God's flock on his heart and is willing to lay down his life for the sheep as the Good Shepherd did—not necessarily in dying for them, but in living for them—as a *living* sacrifice. In all this there is accountability only in one direction—to the Chief Shepherd. No mention is made of any accountability to an electorate.

Early Action—in Acts

The next step in tracing the appointment of elders leads us to the history of the early church as recorded in the Acts of the Apostles. One of these acts was the appointment of elders, as the Apostles Paul and Barnabas did in Acts 14:23, as God's representatives. Again there is no hint of an election.

It is clear from references in Acts 15:2, 4, 6, 22, and 23 that there were already elders in the Jerusalem church as well. They are mentioned in all these scriptures in addition to the apostles, giving us additional evidence of an emerging structure of church administration and government. These elders, in company with the apostles, were consulted on the early problems of church life, making binding decrees without benefit of congregational approval, as seen in the account of the first church council recorded in Acts 15.

More churches—more leaders

The next thread of evidence in the New Testament comes from Paul's instructions to Titus and Timothy in the Pastoral Epistles, especially 1 Timothy and Titus.

When Paul instructs Titus, "This is why I left you in Crete, that you might amend what was defective and *appoint elders* in every town as I directed you . . ." (Tit. 1:5), this moves the appointment of elders down one succeeding step to those whom the apostles themselves designate—in this case, Titus. Continuing through Titus 1:9, we see that the apostle lays down the qualifications of elders or guardians. The word *bishop* here in some versions and *overseer* in others is the same Greek word translated *guardian* in other places mentioned previously.

The instruction in Titus is augmented by that in 1 Timothy 3:1–7 and 1 Peter 5:1–4, and in the emerging church order reflected by these pastoral epistles it seems apparent that these specifications were recorded for future reference, not just for passing interest. So, in the first century and down to the twentieth, we have in these passages God's specification sheet outlining his requirements for leadership in the local church.

Current application

Admittedly, the interpretation of this New Testament data is easier than its application to our current scene. But it would appear by deduction that in each emerging church situation, the twentieth century included, elders should be *appointed*. In the case of existing denominational situations, this appointment should perhaps be made by the denominational authorities responsible for the establishing of the new church. In the case of a nondenominational church it seems obvious that the leadership which the Lord has put together for the founding of that local church should become responsible for leadership in its continuing growth.

In actual cases we have sometimes seen it to be quite apparent who has been appointed by the Lord to assume this responsibility. And in each such situation it has been viewed by those involved as a responsibility that cannot be taken lightly or for the fulfillment of personal ambitions. In questionable cases, however, it would be wise to avoid any conflict of interest inherent in self-appointment by consulting some independent, spiritually minded persons to review the available candidates for local church leadership. This would provide additional safeguard against faulty appointments.

But there is a check even on these careful considerations.

God's Specifications—His Safeguard

The final safeguard is self-evaluation by God's standards, through reviewing the qualifications from the Scriptures themselves as to what God expects from those in positions of spiritual leadership. Simply reading through these Scriptures has a very sobering and salutary effect.

Let's do this right now! Listen to God's "spec sheet" for aspiring leaders:

. . . appoint elders in every city as I directed you, namely, if any man be above reproach, the husband of one wife, having children who believe, not accused of dissipation or rebellion. For the overseer must be above reproach as God's steward, not self-willed, not quick-tempered, not addicted to wine, not pugnacious, not fond of sordid gain, but hospitable, loving what is good, sensible, just, devout, self-controlled, holding fast the faithful word which is in accordance with the teaching, that he may be able both to exhort in sound doctrine and to refute those who contradict (Tit. 1:5–9).

It is trustworthy statement; if any man aspires to the office of overseer, it is a fine work he desires to do. An overseer, then must be above reproach, the husband of one wife, temperate, prudent, respectable, hospitable, able to teach, not addicted to wine or pugnacious, but gentle, uncontentious, free from the love of money. He must be one who manages his own household well, keeping his children under control with all dignity (but if a man does not know how to manage his own household, how will he take care of the church of God?); and not a new convert, lest he become conceited and fall into the condemnation incurred by the devil. And he must have a good reputation with those outside the church, so that he may not fall into reproach and the snare of the devil (1 Tim. 3:1–7, NAS).

Therefore, I exhort the elders among you, as your fellow-elder and witness of the sufferings of Christ, and a partaker also of the glory that is to be revealed, shepherd the flock of God among you, not under compulsion, but voluntarily, according to the will of God; and not for sordid gain, but with eagerness; nor yet as lording it over those allotted to your charge, but proving to be examples to the flock. And when the Chief Shepherd appears, you will receive the unfading crown of glory (1 Pet. 5:1–4, NAS).

Here's what it looks like in summary form with a brief explanation of the terms.

GOD'S SPEC SHEET FOR CHURCH LEADERS

SCRIPTURE	QUALIFICATION	EXPLANATION
	(1) Above reproach	Not open to censure, having unimpeachable integrity.
	(2) Husband of one wife	A one-wife kind of man, not a philanderer (doesn't necessarily rule out widowers or divorced men).
	(3) Having believing children	Children are Christians, not incorrigible or unruly.
	(4) Not self-willed	Not arrogantly self-satisfied.
	(5) Not quick-tempered	Not prone to anger or irascible.
	(6) Not addicted to wine	Not overly fond of wine, or drunken.
	(7) Not pugnacious	Not contentious or quarrelsome.
	(8) Not a money-lover	Not greedy for money.
Titus 1:5–9	(9) Hospitable	A stranger-lover, generous to guests.
	(10) Lover of good	Loving goodness.
	(11) Sensible	Self-controlled, sane, temperate.
	(12) Just	Righteous, upright, aligned with right.
	(13) Devout	Responsible in fulfilling moral obligations to God and man.
	(14) Self-controlled	Restrained, under control.
	(15) Holding fast the Word	Committed to God's Word as authoritative.
	(16) Able to teach sound doctrine	Calling others to wholeness through teaching God's Word.
	(17) Able to refute objections	Convincing those who speak against the truth.

SCRIPTURE	QUALIFICATION	EXPLANATION
Additional from 1 Timothy 3:1-7	(18) Temperate	Calm and collected in spirit, sober.
	(19) Gentle	Fair, equitable, not insisting on his own rights.
	(20) Able to manage household	A good leader in his own family.
	(21) Not a new convert	Not a new Christian.
	(22) Well thought of by outsiders	A good representative of Christ among non-Christians.
Additional from 1 Peter 5:1-4	(23) Willingly, not under compulsion	Not serving against his will.
	(24) According to God (in some Greek texts)	By God's appointment.
	(25) Not for shameful gain	Not money-motivated.
	(26) Not lording it over the flock	Not dominating in his area of ministry (a shepherd is to lead, not *drive* the flock).
	(27) As an example	A pleasure to follow because of his Christian example.
	(28) As accountable to the Chief Shepherd	Motivated by the crown to be gained—authority to reign with Christ.

Do you fit the specs?

After studying these passages, it would be appropriate in assessing leadership potential to ask each man if he is convinced the Lord wants him to serve as God's appointed guardian of the flock. Each man should answer for himself the questions "Am I God's man for this job? Do I qualify?"

Nobody's perfect

As we review the specifications it would seem that no one qualifies—until we reflect that God is not demanding perfection, but rather a heart commitment and a quality of life consistent with the character of Christ. God knows how imperfectly we perform, but he *is* concerned with our heart commitment to his standards and a willingness to be conformed to this pattern, as men under construction. As a matter of fact, he is so serious about this office being fulfilled with honor that he gives special instructions and a solemn charge about the treatment of elders:

> Let the elders who rule well be considered worthy of double honor, especially those who work hard at preaching and teaching. For the Scripture says, "You shall not muzzle the ox while he is threshing," and "The laborer is worthy of his wages." Do not receive an accusation against an elder except on the basis of two or three witnesses. Those [elders] who continue in sin, rebuke in the presence of all, so that the rest also may be fearful of sinning. I solemnly charge you in the presence of God and of Christ Jesus and of His chosen angels, to maintain these principles without bias, doing nothing in a spirit of partiality (1 Tim. 5:17–21, NAS).

In view of this sobering charge from our Lord it seems that we should treat the matter of church government and administration with corresponding seriousness, seeking to fulfill God's pattern, so that ". . . the whole body, joined and knit together by every joint with which it is supplied, when each part is working properly, makes bodily growth and upbuilds itself in love" (Eph. 4:16).

The Administrative Links

We have sought to establish who is in charge and responsible for the proper functioning of the church. Now, so that we don't flee before the imposing demands of the task, let's try to discover how it can work out in practice. Let's look for the administrative links which can tie everything together and give Christ the full and free use of his Body which is the church.

KNEE BONE CONNECTED TO...

CHAPTER THREE

LOOKING FOR MISSING LINKS

People and Principles

"... the whole body, joined and knit together by every joint with which it is supplied, when each part is working properly, makes bodily growth and upbuilds itself in love."—Ephesians 4:16

"When each part is working properly." What does this mean in terms of administrative structure in the church? In the Body of Christ what are the links? Are they people—or principles of operation?

I'd say they are people operating in accord with certain principles just as the joints and tendons of our bodies are members functioning in accord with definite principles.

Administrative Gifts

The members of Christ's body designed to fulfill its administrative needs are those who are *gifted* by the Holy Spirit to fit the required function. For instance, in looking for those who are to rule we must look for the gift of governing. Some people are not suited to govern, since those who govern must somehow have the consent of the governed.

Churches poorly governed soon find one or more of these cases:
(1) a constant need to whip the saints into line by social pressure, harangue, false loyalty pleas, false guilt, etc.
(2) discontented, grumbling people
(3) a fast-disappearing congregation
(4) frustrated leaders who are trying to carry the entire load.
And those with the gift of governing will rule in accord with biblical principles. For example, there must be a discernible *unity of spirit* with other responsible leaders, a joint commitment to know the mind of Christ on a matter, not just to settle for a majority vote. This calls for *openness* of heart, *honesty* in prayer and *unanimity* in action.

Governing

How do we recognize the gift of governing? We do it by looking for men who are easy to follow, men with orderly minds and orderly lives. And we look for men of good report. This does not equate with popularity or view just an affable personality, but encompasses a quality of life that calls out men's willingness to follow.

Leadership

But there are other administrative functions besides governing. The church has many leadership needs. Here too we look for those who have been gifted by the Holy Spirit to fulfill these equally vital functions in the Body, for example, leading meetings, worship services, etc. We have all experienced the painful torture of groaning through a service where the leader was scared, self-conscious, and painfully uncomfortable. We became uncomfortable with him and alternately felt sorry for him, prayed, and wished he would shut up and sit down. On the other hand, a gifted leader is so unobtrusive as to blend into the scenery, and is used of God to draw out our hearts to worship, pray, sing and rejoice in a genuine experience of fellowship wrought by the Holy Spirit.

Ministrivia

A third kind of administrative person is the one gifted by God to perform the multitude of "household chores" needed to keep the church running smoothly. The sixth chapter of Acts records the early appointment of those whom we call deacons,* from the Greek word *diakonos*. In this case their function was to distribute the food among the saints, or to wait on tables. And as we read the account we find they were to be men of high spiritual qualifications, so this was no second-rate, demeaning job. They were to be "men of good report, full of wisdom, full of the Holy Spirit." Every church has many deacons, not always in terms of title or office, but as fulfilling a needed function in the Body. As in Acts, this is no less important an assignment than the appointment given to those who are to rule. All the gifts and ministries are important to the operation of the Body!

People, functioning in the Body of Christ according to God-given *principles*—that's the way it should be, not one man (the pastor) expected to do everything.

The three basic administrative functions described above are identifiable in Scripture as seen in this chart:

---

*A fuller consideration of deacons is included in chapter 8.

GIFT	GREEK WORD	SCRIPTURE	DESCRIPTION
Governing	*kubernesis*	1 Cor. 12:28	To guide or direct, as a pilot does a ship
Leadership	*proistemi*	Romans 12:8	To "stand before" in the sense of taking the lead
Service	*diakonia*	Romans 12:7	"Household chores" in the family household of God

Faith

Then there is the gift of faith, and what an asset are those who exhibit this gift! A dear friend whom I learned to call Caleb because he is so like the Old Testament character by that name (Num. 13:30) is a wonderful example. Of the Old Testament Caleb the Scripture records at least five times, "He wholly followed the Lord." And so it was with my friend. Whenever we confronted seemingly impossible situations he would say, "I wonder how the Lord is going to get us through this one. Let's find out!" Many times when we could see no financial support for a move we believed the Lord wanted us to make he would ask, "Do we really have the mind of the Lord on this? If we do, let's go ahead and expect him to supply the funds." At that point, not only he but ten other men on the governing board sought very seriously to gain that sense of peace and unanimity that gave the go-ahead on the action. As a result, never has the Lord failed to supply our needs—even though we embarked on many ventures with no human assurance that the funds would be forthcoming. All this came about without our ever soliciting a pledge!

Wisdom

Right here we need to mention the gift of "the word of wisdom" as mentioned in 1 Corinthians 12. Have you ever had the experience in a board or committee meeting where everyone thought and discussed and argued back and forth seemingly for hours without reaching a decision? It's very discouraging, to say the least. At such a point, in the case I have in mind, one elder, who had been quietly listening and thinking but not contributing much to the discussion, spoke up. "What do you think of this approach to the problem?" And he proceeded to spell out the exact solution which was needed, but which nobody had recognized until then. The response was immediate and positive. This man had exercised the gift of wisdom, or more properly, the word of wisdom, at a time when it was particularly needed and appreciated.

We need men in Christian leadership roles who exemplify these attributes, for without them the church flounders. But do we always see leaders chosen on the basis of gifts of the Spirit? Too often they are chosen on the basis of a different kind of gifts—the monetary ones they give to the church. Putting it another way, the church needs men with gifts of leadership and administration who are able to think through, plan, organize, and keep things in manageable order.

Watching the Plan Work

Some years ago when we experienced a lack in these areas of ministry, we began to pray that the Lord would give us men to fill these needs, or help us to discover men we already had in our midst but so far had failed to recognize.

This, incidentally, is what we believe the Apostle had in mind when he said in 1 Corinthians 12:31, "But earnestly desire the best gifts." Since spiritual gifts are given according to the sovereign will of the Holy Spirit, we are not to desire for ourselves, as individuals, gifts we do not have, but we *are* to desire the greater gifts to fulfill the needs of the local church body. The verb here is plural, "you-all desire the best gifts." This is especially clear when we recognize that spiritual gifts are "for the *common* good" (1 Cor. 12:7) and, "Let all things be done for edification," that is, building up the Body (1 Cor. 14:26b).

So we prayed and expectantly examined the men God had in our focus. And sure enough, there they were! One was the youngest elder on the board, but the one (because of his gifts) whom

God gave the responsibility of being chairman. This seems foolish, doesn't it, in terms of our usual way of thinking. But this man proved to be the instrument God used to promote the kind of action that is needed in the governing body of a church.

Over a period of time, and in spite of many mistakes, the example of this one man led us, through his heart commitment to be God's man, to the place where things began to be put in good order. Every elder was evaluated by his peers as to performance and gifts. We moved from there to the evaluation of every staff man as to how well he was fulfilling his assignment and where he really fit in the ministry of the church. The results of this latter evaluation were published in the church bulletin in a form something like this:

TO OUR CHURCH FAMILY . . .

The elders of a local church have a very demanding assignment— *to find the mind of the Lord*, the great Head of the church, as to the direction and functioning of the church. As part of this assignment, during the past several months the Board of Elders has carefully reviewed each of the major staff functions as to where the Lord wants to lead us in the future. Thoughtful consideration was given to current needs, future opportunities, and the spiritual gifts of each staff member. After much prayer and thorough discussion, the Board unanimously approved the following directives:

Pastor X

Pastor X is appointed to a prophetic ministry (this means illuminating the Scripture) to the local body and to be our ambassador to the Body of Christ at large. We believe that his gifts and ministry are such that the Lord wants to use them toward prospering the whole Christian community. He is directed to reduce to writing his expository teachings given at the home base so that this material can be effectively distributed to the Body at large. We especially want him to have time to develop new lines of study and make the results available to all of us.

Pastor Z

Pastor Z is appointed the Pastor/Leader of the staff to work in a relationship of Advisor and Counselor to the general operations of this local church. He is directed to pursue a teaching/training ministry particularly aimed at developing leadership. He is directed to limit his counseling to premarital counseling only—taking on no other types of counseling (this is necessary to respect his health situation), and is also directed to continue his documentation of expository research and significant material presented in connection with our ministry locally. Also he will assist in some of the administrative activities.

Pastor W

Pastor W has been appointed to an expository teaching ministry from the pulpit (in conjunction with Pastor X), and to teach, counsel, and work in the area of a couples' ministry. He is also directed to continue his activity in disciplining men and is encouraged to pursue and develop home churches composed of small groups meeting in different locations throughout the area.

Pastor V

The Board believes strongly that Pastor V needs to develop his own gifts and assume responsibility wider than his present ministry and that his situation at this local church inhibits this process. So he was asked, for the sake of all the Lord wants to do through him, to seek a new situation. This action is based strictly on his best interests, and we want it clearly understood he is *not* being discharged. He is currently looking at opportunities the Lord has for him in areas outside of this local church. When he has found exactly the right place the Lord has for him, he will leave his responsibilities here. Until this is accomplished, he is directed to continue his responsibilities overseeing his present ministry, including the summer programs.

Pastor T

The Board has directed that he continue his responsibility for the Body Life ministry. On June 15, he leaves the high school ministry to undertake a ministry of teaching in adult electives and evangelistic home Bible studies. He is directed to employ his illustrative gift to assist the audio/visual and Christian education ministries.

Pastor J

Pastor J has accepted the Board's invitation to become the pastor overseeing the college ministry. On May 1, he began on a formal basis to continue the ministry he has been carrying as a second-year intern under the leadership of Pastor W.

Pastor R

Pastor R has accepted an invitation from the Board to become a pastor overseeing the high school ministry here. On June 15 he will formally start this ministry and until that time he will be finishing his seminary work.

Pastor P

Pastor P has accepted the invitation of the Board to begin as Pastor/Administrator. This involves overseeing administrative matters connected with the general operation of this local church. (He will work in concert with Pastor Z in many of these areas.) He is directed to take these responsibilities beginning May 1, some of which he has been carrying as a consultant during the past year. He is also directed to continue his teaching ministry in the adult area.

Intern Coordinator and Publication Director

The Board has directed that they continue their activities essentially as before.

The Board is also concerned that pastors be available to meet counseling needs, crisis situations, hospital calls, weddings, funerals, etc. To accomplish this aim, Pastors P and Z are to be available (one or the other) throughout the week at the church office to see that these needs are met. This doesn't mean that these men will do it all themselves, but they are to see that some member of the pastoral staff is alerted to meet these needs.

The following lists all of our staff. [There followed a listing of all secretarial, accounting and facilities personnel.] Much could be said about those who contribute such a great deal behind the scenes. We just thank the Lord for giving us this operating staff of wonderful secretaries who faithfully and cheerfully carry many diverse responsibilities. The same is true of our facilities personnel.

As our congregation has grown, so our staff has grown to minister to the larger body of believers, but we need to recall that our Lord's directive is still the same. "And his gifts were that . . . some should be pastors and teachers *toward the equipping of the saints for their work of ministry* . . ." (Eph. 4:11–12).

And "All of you are brothers"—no clergy, no hierarchy—all ONE in Christ!

We ask for your continued support and prayers for our staff, board and ministry here as we all serve the Lord together as members of His Body.

THE BOARD OF ELDERS

This is a unique document, wrought by the Lord out of the crucible of head-to-head confrontations in many long meetings, agonizing heart-searching, and genuinely dependent prayer. It represents the unity of the Spirit demonstrated in the lives of strong-willed, hard-headed men—but God's men, committed to the Lordship of Christ in their lives and in the life of the church. And what a glory it is to see!

You mean that God's plan for governing the church really works?

The answer is a resounding yes!—as long as we allow Christ to be who He is, Lord and Head. Incidentally, the second man God gave us as the result of prayer was Pastor P, the Pastor/Administrator, whose gifts and insight have shaped things up like never before!

It's most exciting to recall that Pastor X (the one who would be called the senior pastor in most churches) graciously responded to the elders' directive to relinquish the administrative leadership of the staff to a fellow pastor who has had no seminary training. This was especially meaningful in that all of the Board were spiritually less mature than he, and they were led by a young salesman who grew up under his ministry.

How could this happen? Pastor X is truly humble, and more than that, he recognizes the validity of spiritual gifts and their function. But perhaps the most important point: he is subject to the authority of the elders and is committed to God's ability to govern a local church through his appointed leaders.

What a picture of mingled grace, conviction, and obedience!

We could multiply examples of how ". . . the whole body, joined and knit together by every joint with which it is supplied, when each part is working properly, makes bodily growth and upbuilds itself in love" (Eph. 4:16). But the Lord is still writing the story and he wants you to write the next chapter in your church!

It may be helpful in specific situations to review the following chart compiled from the biblical information on qualifications for spiritual leadership and spiritual gifts. We found this an excellent way to take a spiritual inventory of present and potential leadership.

Further information on spiritual gifts and ministries is included in the study of 1 Corinthians 12 entitled "Saints Alive!" (Appendix B).

LEADERSHIP EVALUATION FOR_____

"But let each one examine his own work, and then he will have reason for boasting in regard to himself alone, and not in regard to another. For each one shall bear his own load" (Gal. 6:4–5, NAS).

Note: These qualities are to characterize the man's life style. Perfection is not in view. The Lord knows we are all "men under construction."

			Check One		
			Yes	No	??
#1 **Essential** →		1. Born-again believer (holy) *John 3:3, 10;* "Without me you can do *Titus 1:8, 2:12;* nothing" *John 15:5*			
QUALIFICATIONS FOR SPIRITUAL LEADERSHIP Titus, 1 Timothy 3: "Must be . . ."	*1 Tim. 3:2*	2. Above reproach *Titus 1:6* Not open to justifiable accusations			
		3. A "one wife" husband, if married *Titus 1:6* Not a polygamist or philanderer			
		4. Temperate *Eph. 5:15* Not living thoughtlessly			
		5. Sensible *Titus 1:8* Sober-minded			
		6. Respectable Orderly, disciplined life			
		7. Hospitable *Titus 1:8* Given to hospitality			
		8. Apt at teaching Able and capable to teach; also teachable			
	1 Tim. 3:3	9. Not addicted to wine Not a drunkard, not given to excess			
		10. Nonviolent Physically gentle, noncombative			
		11. Not quarrelsome Not self-willed or contentious			
		12. Free from money greed Not money-hungry, not loving money			
		13. Managing home and children *1 Tim 3:4–5* Home and children under control with dignity			
		14. Not a novice *1 Tim. 3:6* Not a beginner in the faith (new Christian)			
		15. Good reputation with unsaved *1 Tim. 3:7* Well thought of by non-Christians in community			
		16. Fair-minded *Titus 1:8, 2:12* Just			
		17. Self-controlled *Titus 1:7* Not quick-tempered			

		Yes	No	??
SPIRITUAL WORKING GIFTS — Every believer has at least one, and perhaps more	1. Wisdom *1 Cor 12:8* To understand how truth applies			
	2. Knowledge *1 Cor. 12:8* Ability to recognize and *1 Cor. 12:8* systemize spiritual facts			
	3. Faith *1 Cor. 12:9* Vision to see what God wants done; courage and faith to tackle and accomplish "impossible"			
	4. Prophecy *1 Cor. 12:10, 14:3, 24–25* A spokesman for God, using God's Word, causing it to shine; moving people to worship			
	5. Discernment *1 Cor. 12:10* Able to distinguish between truth and error, spot subtle forms of phoniness			
	6. Helps *1 Cor. 18:28; Rom. 12:7* Lending a needed helping hand, support; being moved by pity to give aid, mercy			
	7. Teaching *Rom. 12:7; 1 Cor. 12:28* Ability to give spiritual instruction resulting in someone learning truth of God			
	8. Serving *Rom. 12:7* Caring for details, from "household servant"			
	9. Leadership *Rom. 12:8* Standing before and leading; chairing committees, etc.			
	10. Guiding *1 Cor. 12:28* Standing behind and steering; guiding spiritual affairs			
	11. Giving *Rom. 12:8* Sensitive to needs; all assets available for God's use			
	12. Exhortation *Rom. 12:8* Ability to encourage, comfort, motivate people with God's Word; get people moving			

(Chart compiled by Walt McCuistion, used by permission.)

OKAY, OKAY, YOU GUYS!

CHAPTER FOUR

LEADERSHIP . . . OR DOMINATION?

How should the structure of the governing body of a local church be set up? Undoubtedly there is room for a wide divergence of opinion on this subject. Granting this, let's examine both the biblical and practical reasons we might use as guidelines for an idealized pattern.

A Board—or Just Bored?

I remember once telling my pastor I would never again serve on the board of a church. I was bored, fed up, and plain disgusted with the petty, unchristian, and sometimes ridiculous antics we

44

groaned through. Our action had better be more vital than that! Otherwise we have bored boards.

But first, how *many* boards should we have? May we suggest from practical considerations that the answer is one. The reason seems obvious: only one board can assume the *responsibility* for governing. Any other way results in confusion, because it sets up rival authorities. Certainly the one responsible board can set up committees and delegate responsibilities for various areas of ministry, but the overall *accountability* is nontransferable.

A division of authority along the typical lines of spiritual, temporal, and financial realms invariably seems to breed strife. That's because the basis of division is false: it implies that financial matters and mundane housekeeping chores are not considered "spiritual." This runs counter to the principles of Scripture, for in 1 Corinthians the inspired writer moves without a pause from the obviously spiritual consideration of the resurrection (Chap. 15) to the matter of finances (16:1–4). Also, as previously cited in Acts 6, spiritual qualities were required in men called to the household chore of waiting on tables. Neither of these matters is considered less spiritual than more deeply "theological" issues; all are to be handled in the power of an indwelling Lord and under the direction of the Spirit of God.

A more biblical division of labor is set forth in the view that the elders are responsible before God to rule, and in addition there are many functioning deacons (household servants) who are called of God to function in equally important and vital ways— but without any *ruling* authority whatever.

The key issue seems to be: *who are the ones God will call to account for the governing responsibilities?* They are the ones described in the Word as guardians or overseers. They alone have ruling authority—and accountability.

Now, based on this reasoning, if we assume that one board is best, how should it function? And on what biblical principles?

Brothers

What's the setup?

Our Lord lays out the basic concept which answers this question in the simple phrase, "you are all brothers."

If we read the statement beginning in Matthew 23 in this context, we see that the Lord Jesus is saying, "Don't emulate the scribes and Pharisees, for they have set themselves up above the masses, and love the honor and praise of men, including being called 'Rabbi.' " He is cautioning us not to look for exalted titles and ranks, for we are all just brothers in a great, big family—God's family. And there are no ranks and titles in a family! So he says: ". . . you are not to be called Rabbi: for you have one teacher, *and you are all brethren*. And call no man your father on earth, for you have one Father, who is in heaven. Neither be called masters, for you have one master, the Christ" (Matt. 23:8–10).

This means that every man on the governing board of a church should have equal standing and authority. The pastor and/or paid staff should not dominate the action. Major decisions (and perhaps even some minor ones, when necessary) should be made on the basis of unanimity with each man exercising a single vote.

If you question the workability of this rule, let me give you an example of how it works. As a Board of Elders we were considering the important matter of calling a youth pastor. The need was pressing. Our young people needed a shepherd; their parents were concerned; and so were we. We interviewed a young man, discussed his potential leadership and other qualifications, assessed his spiritual life and maturity, and everyone agreed we should call him—except one elder!

Since we were committed to unanimous action, the heat was on. Was the majority right, or was the one odd-ball holdout right? Who really had the mind of the Lord?

It could be either way, so we rested the matter back on the Lord for further clarity of understanding and direction. We prayed, and talked, and thought and prayed some more. And as you can imagine, the pressure was really on the holdout. The longer it went the more he thought "I must be wrong on this. I couldn't be the only one out of all these guys to have the clue from the Lord." So he finally succumbed and said, "Okay, let's go ahead and call him." But it wasn't over a couple of months until *all* of us realized we had made a mistake. The man we called did not handle the ministry satisfactorily, and we faced the painful necessity of letting him go.

That was an important lesson none of us have forgotten. We learned that the Lord may be trying to tell us something through the one man who does not concur in the action. And we'd better not pressure him into feeling he is so far out of it that *he* is the unspiritual and insensitive one. In this one case the safeguard didn't work very well—but only because we panicked! In many other cases it has saved the frustration and embarrassment of making hasty, wrong decisions.

Unanimity is a great safeguard against precipitous and premature decision. Why? Because it makes us truly dependent on the Lord to pray it through in patient waiting on him. The eternal God is never in a hurry even when we are. And most of us sit pretty close to the panic button—sometimes *on* it.

We need to give each leader unhurried and unharried freedom to respond to Christ as Head. Discussion without pressure, logic without coercion is the way to go.

Who takes the lead?

Okay, so we're all *brothers*. And we do need the safeguard of *unanimity*. Doesn't *someone* have to exercise leadership in the action of a ruling board? Leadership, yes—domination, no. Leadership is needed, and in order to balance the obvious advantage staff men have (because of spending all their working hours in the ministry of the local church) the leadership roles should be given to the non-staff elders. In one church we know there is an unwritten but well-established rule that no staff man may hold office on the board. That is, non-staff people act as chairman, vice-chairman, secretary, treasurer, and other officers. On the other hand, *every* elder has an assigned area of responsibility in the ministry. These ideas help to maintain the equality of "brothers" in practical terms.

Neither are the staff personnel to be considered as "employees" of the board. There are employment considerations to be made, in view of tax laws, vacation policies, insurance programs, and so on; but the attitude "He's my brother" should be reflected as the background feature of the relationship between staff and non-staff elders.

Clergy—What's That?

Where do we get the idea of a "clergy" anyway? Certainly not from the Bible! It's more likely that an enemy has planted this idea in our minds, because it has done so much to reverse God's order of things in the church. Even in enlightened quarters the idea persists that only the paid minister can perform certain church functions like baptizing, serving communion, and visiting the sick. In recent situations which we have observed, various Christians have complained bitterly because the "senior pastor" was not able to visit their loved one, conduct the funeral for a member of their family, or other such services, even when all kinds of loving care were being expressed by other members of the Body. And when in the course of planning a men's conference we suggested that some of the ordinary "civilians" conduct a communion service, one man said, "Oh, can we do that?"

I often wonder why we don't think back to the first-century church scene: Who conducted the early communion services? From what seminary did they graduate? What denominational sanction did they have? Was it not the rough hands of unlettered fishermen who broke the bread of those early days? Or perhaps it was the cleansed heart of a converted publican that expressed thanks for "the blood of the new covenant shed for the remission of sins."

What seminary did you attend?

There are only three schools I can think of from which those early disciples could have graduated:
(1) The Jewish instructional centers like that of Gamaliel, from which they could hardly have learned Christian truth,
(2) the "School of Despair" as Ian Thomas describes it, otherwise known as the "School of Hard Knocks,"
(3) or "St. Mary's College"—the one which Mary of Bethany established when she sat at the feet of Jesus.

This third school is the one which every Christian must attend —and the one from which none of us ever graduates. It's the source from which the wisest, most distinguished pastor or Bible scholar as well as the lowliest, least-recognized Christian must draw. "You are all brothers." In God's eyes there are no ranks, no hierarchy, no clergy—just Christ's men and women with different gifts and ministries, loving one another and caring for each other in Christ's name!

How about seminaries?

Lest you think I am against seminaries, let me hasten to correct that impression. Good seminaries perform a very necessary function, giving men the tools for becoming good Bible expositors and building their background of understanding in theology, besides the disciplining of thought and study habits. But placing confidence in our academic excellence or degrees is never an acceptable substitute for being taught of God and walking in genuine dependence on the available resources of our Risen Lord!

I hope the point is obvious: Our Lord has more than one way to educate his men. Some he teaches through a seminary; others learn from faithful pastors and Bible teachers. But *all* must respond to *his personal instruction*, not just for three or four years, but for a lifetime. Make no mistake—God puts no premium on ignorance, but he reserves the right to be the Master Teacher.

A seminary education (or an engineering degree) is simply a license to look for a job and start using what we've learned in productive employment—under the personal tutoring of the Spirit of God. Academic truth has no real value until it becomes *applied* truth.

In a church I know, one pastor has earned his doctorate in theology, while his co-pastor has never attended seminary. As I facetiously tell them: one is educated beyond his intelligence and the other is hardly even educated. The beauty of this situation is that both men are completely free and uninhibited about it! But both men are educated. Their education came through different channels, but both are taught of God and fulfilling an effective ministry side by side—with no strain about their educational disparity.

When the "untaught" man was introduced to the congregation he was to serve, the "doctor" asked him, "What formal theological training have you had?" (This was in a Sunday service on an entirely unrehearsed basis.) The slightly startled reply was, "I've never had any," followed by the next question, "Then what makes you think you can be a pastor to these people?" I'm sure there must have been a long pause at this point—and then the thoughtful response, "I know I'm not adequate in myself to think I could make it, but I have the assurance from God that he has qualified us to be ministers of a new covenant. That's the basis of my confidence."

You say, "Wasn't this interview kind of risky?" Sure it was, but the "educated" pastor knew his man and on that basis proceeded with confidence. And can you imagine how this set up the new man with the people? Their hearts were enlisted to move with him in the fulfillment of his ministry, and they were at the same time encouraged to think, "If the Lord can teach this man and use him—without formal training—maybe there's hope for me!"

The point is this: the real qualifications for ministry are spiritual, not scholastic.

The Lord seems to delight in shaking up the theological world by revealing truth to unlikely candidates like A. W. Tozer, or to a British Army officer like Major Ian Thomas. God, it seems, is well able to make his own channels for disseminating his truth. I say this only that we might let God be God, and not try to press him into our academic molds. I've noticed he easily avoids our misguided attempts to package him and sell him under our labels.

How about denominations?

The same idea applies to the view one takes toward denominations. I suggest that denominationalism is an attitude of mind rather than a mere attachment to a name. It's possible for a nondenominational church to be permeated with such an avid sectarian spirit that its people are more denominational than those in the denominational framework. The same is possible regarding our view of the pastorate: I have known some who are so anticlerical that they have made a "clergy" of the laity. What a beautifully simple word our Lord uses to resolve all of this: "You are all brothers."

Communications and P.R.

Communication and public relations are essential in any local church scene, simply because *love communicates*. This means that we need to spend enough time and express enough concern to begin to know each other and show that we care. This should take place on every level of church life: in the governing board, among the staff and extending to and through the whole congregation.

At a board meeting I attended not long ago the leader chairing the meeting (not the board chairman, but one of the men being given the opportunity to act in that capacity as a learning experience) asked the question, "Is anyone hurting?" This invitation for us to share areas of need with the other men resulted in silence for a bit as we all thought through our situations. Then the first elder (whom we'll call Len) said, "Well, if you fellows aren't hurting, I am! I came home late tonight after one of those impossible, hectic days at work, had a spat with my wife and slammed the door after me as I left the house to come to this meeting. And I feel rotten about it."

Well, that opened us up! Other elders began to share their needs, along with their victories, and praise. When we had finished praying for each of the men, one of the elders said to Len, "We'll take a five-minute break. How about calling your wife?" When the meeting resumed, Len was all smiles and ready to lead with joy instead of a heavy heart.

On another occasion one of the pastoral staff came to a meeting with a sad face and eyes red-rimmed from weeping. He shared a deep concern which was affecting his whole family and possibly his ministry. The response was such a ministry of love from all the elders that we could only express our hearts to the Lord with a communion service! So the cookies and punch on hand for refreshments became the elements of a "holy" communion which could only bring delight to the heart of the One whose death and life it portrays.

Do you see this picture? Here are ordinary "civilian-type" Chris
tians ministering to a pastor! Here are brothers together, com·
municating Christian love.

In our all-day staff meetings the most important ingredients are
hearing from the Lord, through His Word; sharing our personal
needs and heart concerns; and praying for one another concerning
personal and ministry needs. Only after that are we ready to
function as a team under the Lord's direction—to think through
and develop plans and programs to equip His saints for their
ministry.

A classic illustration of a board ministering in love occurred
with a pastor I know. This pastor had a heart attack, for which
the only attributable causes were stress and fatigue. So knowing
how difficult it had always been for him to say no to any appeal
for help, his board of elders issued orders to limit his activity,
taking steps to guard his health. The board chairman personally
became the guardian of his ministry activities. And all this occurred after three months' absence of the pastor and in the face of
multiple problems of both personal and management nature in
the life of the board chairman. That's what I call T.L.C. (Tender
Loving Care) to the nth degree!

Then there is the case of Pastor V on page 38. This man was
asked to seek another place of ministry, not for failure to perform,
but to develop his own potentials. At least three elders on the
board that took this action were among Pastor V's closest friends.
Can you see some of the possibilities of misunderstanding in this?
The suspicions of double-cross and betrayal? This was a costly
decision—running the risk of misunderstanding and possible loss
of friendship—for love's sake.

Communication is a necessary feature of life where love is
involved, maintaining the freshness of that love relationship and
the clarity of understanding that creates harmony of thought and
unity of action.

How about the rest?

Now that we've considered communications on a staff and
board level, what about public relations with the rest of the local
body?

This is frequently an area of weakness, especially in a church not committed to democratic or congregational lines of government. But if the elders expect people to cooperate with the lines of action they believe were received directly from "Headquarters," then the people must be included in the communications loop. This can be done in a number of ways:

(1) through published information in the church bulletin and/or newsletter;

(2) through representatives of the congregation meeting with the board as advisors;

(3) by inviting leaders of the various ministries of the church to meet with the board for sharing of information and reporting;

(4) by appointing liaison representatives from the board to each ministry group in the church;

(5) by appointing advisors to the board from the various segments of church life, particularly the youth and children's areas of ministry (and any other that might be more remote and thus tend to be neglected);

(6) by honestly considering and heeding criticism from the people and by maintaining a consistent, ongoing assessment of congregational needs.

There are undoubtedly many more ways, but they will only be apparent as we learn to exercise that thoughtful consideration generated out of genuine love. For *love communicates*. And that's how we came to know the Lord of love, through the costly communication of the Cross and the Word of the Cross.

The leadership of love is easy to follow!

GETTING IN THE GAME

CHAPTER FIVE

GOD GIVES PASTORS
—FOR WHAT?

A Model Pastor

God gives pastors—for what?

It's strange to me that in thinking through the answer to this question the last thing that occurred to me was that we have a Model. My mind went through the whole catalog of methods and programs before the light dawned: How about the Good Shepherd? Don't we have in him the one perfect portrayal of what a pastor should be? How did he operate?

Number one—

Well, first, he kept his own life in order. In his own words:
". . . I do nothing on my own authority but speak thus as the

Father taught me . . . for I always do what is pleasing to him" (John 8:28–29).

That's a good place for pastors to start!

Number two—

He had a heart of compassion for his flock: "When Jesus saw her weeping . . . he was deeply moved in spirit and troubled; and . . . Jesus wept (John 11:33–35). In the Greek of this text it is apparent that our Lord's first emotion was a seething anger at the awful devastation and frustration that death brings; then there was a sudden, quiet flow of tears as his pastor's heart identified with his friends in their grief and unbelief. This picture is especially beautiful when we remember that Jesus then proceeded to bring his friend Lazarus back to life.

Number three—

He took his disciples with him, to let them see his actions and reactions in every kind of situation. There was no cover-up; they lived with him and thus had opportunity to observe the intimate detail of his life and ministry. Oh, yes, he puzzled them and stretched their minds and their faith to try to understand him. But what a way to learn!

Number four—

He taught them the truth about life. He satisfied their deepest hunger, by leading them to green pastures and still waters. He led them in right paths! And what does God's flock need more than these?

How sad that we should offer them gimmicks and gadgets—the Mickey Mouse approaches and Band-Aid solutions to the deep problems of human life. Only the Word of life will suffice to meet the deep needs of the human heart. How dare we give "sermons" and neat little essays of human opinion instead of proclaiming the Word in clarity and power.

Jesus was a living exposition of life in what he did and what he

said. Can we substitute another way and claim to be Christ's men?
Have you noticed how many times our Lord said, "Follow me!"
in the Gospels? Perhaps that's the word we need to begin to take
seriously. He's the model—*especially* for pastors.

But, you say, we need a modern example so we can see how
these principles work out in practice—now. Okay, let's look at
some, for in my life span I've seen all kinds of evidence, both
positive and negative, that we can follow, even twenty centuries
later. But we've barely begun to see and employ all the practical
value of his way.

Some Basic Essentials for the Twentieth Century

Let's look at some of the ways we *have* discovered:

• Keep a constant flow of teaching on the New Covenant
concept that we are totally inadequate in ourselves, but completely adequate as we trust in the sufficiency of our indwelling
Lord. This is the mainline teaching throughout the Bible—
how to walk by faith and enjoy victory through Christ. And
it's there in every portion of Scripture.

• Complement the central expository ministry from the pulpit
with life-related fellowship in sharing type activities as described by Ray Stedman in his book *Body Life*. Add to this
plenty of sharing in Sunday school classes and home meetings,
where there is ample dialogue for opening up the key issues
that are bothering people. There is sharing together in both
learning and caring in this kind of atmosphere.

Show and tell

• Provide all kinds of how-to-do-it opportunities in which people
can be shown as well as told how to function in real situations.
This means we offer practice teaching situations, then real-life
teaching ministries; training on how to witness, then actual
witnessing together to people whose eternal destiny is at stake;
counselor training, then opportunities to really help people in
deep need. There's no way this approach can be just an
academic exercise or "spectator sport."

Making disciples

•Have enough concern and commitment to actually disciple our leaders and workers instead of handing them a book and turning them loose on their own. This means a commitment and priority of spending time with them, just as our Lord with his own. (See Dave Roper's brief, "Making Disciples," in Appendix A.)

•And most important—keep our own fellowship fresh and sweet with our Lord by hearing and obeying his Word. There's no way we can be part of the answer when we're part of the problem. Why? Because we have no power in ourselves to effect redemptive changes in people. Our Lord said, "Apart from me you can do nothing" (John 15:5).

Discovering gifts

We can also, as pastors, help people discover their gifts by teaching what spiritual gifts are and giving opportunity to explore various possibilities of ministry. (See "Saints Alive!," Appendix A, and *Body Life*, already referred to, for guidelines on this.)

Research data

We can also do research and teaching on problem areas like abortion, marriage and divorce, women's lib, and other current concerns. It's most helpful if the pastoral staff can lead out in this research together, then teach their conclusions to other leaders and teachers. Pastor David Roper's brief on Principles of the Ministry in Appendix C is a good example.

Resource help

Much can be done to help our people in their personal lives and ministries if we will be available to consult with them on interpretive problems, counseling situations, and the like. We should be ready to back up their ministries any way we can. Incidentally, we have found that much of this can be done on the telephone.

The Big Burner

Total Christian education should be our goal. As one of my colleagues says, it's like a big burner: the expository pulpit ministry is the center of the burner, and the complementary efforts with their greater participation possibilities form the outer rings of the burner. This is the air-conditioning system of a church, maintaining a warm atmosphere and a climate conducive to spiritual health and growth.

Let's light up the Big Burner, not to make things hot for everyone, but to warm up the saints and condition the atmosphere. It can be the means by which we really hear from God, setting the whole tone of the ministry.

In order to do this we must get back to the kind of expository teaching that is dedicated to lifting out and presenting the true sense of the text so that God can reach our wills through our minds. This demands forthright declaration of truth in clarity and power. No wonder the early apostles decided they should "give themselves to the word of God and prayer" (Acts 6:4).

And dialogue, not monologue

Let's use all the creative imagination we possess to provide lots of sharing—of needs and supply, of doubts and faith, of questions and knowledge, of hurts and healing. Let's be willing to listen, talk, probe, debate, yield out of love, or stand firm on convictions in order that ". . . speaking the truth in love, we may grow up in every way into him who is the head, into Christ, from whom the whole body knit together by every joint with which it is supplied, when each part is working properly, *makes bodily growth and upbuilds itself in love*" (Eph. 4:15-16).

God's Gift to the Church—Pastors?

One of my fellow pastors said one time: "The best thing that could happen to the church is for all the pastors to be put in jail." Obviously this was said somewhat facetiously and not because he hates pastors, for he is one. The point is that if all the pastors were removed from the scene, Christians would *have* to count on the ministry of the saints and so learn to trust the Lord to work *through them,* not just the paid professionals. How far we have strayed from God's original plan for the church, because in most churches the pastor is almost the whole show!

Actually, pastors *are God's gift to the church,* and his intentions were good. Along with apostles, prophets and evangelists, ". . . his gifts were that some should be . . . pastors and teachers toward the fitting out of the saints [all God's people] for a work of ministry" (Eph. 4:12, a literal rendering). In other words, a pastor is sort of a "playing coach," not just on the bench, but in the game—not just telling the team what to do, but doing it with them so as to show them how.

This is quite different from what happens so often.

To summarize

Pastors should be training people to:

• discover their gifts,
• learn how to study the Bible,
• learn to be counselors,
• learn to teach,
• learn how to evangelize,
• learn to recognize and defeat the Christians' enemies,
• but most of all, how to live in liberty and triumph through Christ: in their families, in their work, among worldlings, and in the Christian body.

Know any pastors? Are *you* one?

Will the Real Pastor Please Stand Up?

I am often asked, "How many pastors do you have in your church? And the only honest answer I can give is "a lot." If they are talking about paid professionals I could give them a number, but if they are dealing with reality, I can't be specific. In reality we do have a lot.

Who is the pastor to the preschool kids? Certainly none of the paid pros are. Most of us never even see the preschoolers unless we happen to have one in our family. Yet the preschoolers don't lack pastors.

I love to tell the story of a young woman I know who was brought up shooting dice with "the boys" in the back room of a bar. Through the loving concern of a relative she got into an adult Bible class and discovered the joy of a personal relationship with Jesus Christ. Some time later when she heard a plea for help in a preschool class, she volunteered to help in the emergency. But she remained in that ministry for many years and became the department director for the whole preschool ministry. Who was the real pastor to preschoolers? It's not hard to see that it was this young woman. She and a corps of other teachers were the real shepherds of this "little flock."

Elders are also pastors. Every man in ruling authority must have his personal ministry and area of pastoral care.

"Brothers" again

The only distinction I can see between the paid pastoral staff and the other pastors in the church is that some are financially supported to free them to devote their full time to their pastoral responsibilities. It's great for people to understand it that way: that all of us called to a pastoral ministry, whether paid or volunteer, are co-pastors in caring for God's flock.

God gave many to be pastors and teachers. "Every good endowment and every perfect gift is from above, coming down from the Father of lights with whom there is no variation or shadow due to change" (James 1:17).

PENETRATING THE SMOKE-BARRIER

CHAPTER SIX

WORKERS TOGETHER WITH GOD

How does one get Christians to work *together* toward God's appointed goals? This is a big question, but one very natural way to see this happen is to foster the idea of home Bible classes as they can be used to reach the community with the gospel of Christ.

The Church in the World

Some time ago there appeared in *Decision* magazine an article by Dr. Howard Hendricks of Dallas Theological Seminary which beautifully describes the ministry of home Bible studies. It goes like this:

I well remember my introduction to the home Bible class movement. A church leader invited me to take her class while she was
out of the city. I arrived at the house, opened the front door and
found the living room filled with smoke.

"Oh, I'm awfully sorry. I have the wrong house," I said.

"No, you're Mr. Hendricks, aren't you?" they said. "We're
waiting for the Bible study. Come on in."

"Here?"

"Here."

A female dreadnought was sitting on the divan, taking a drag,
and I still recall the Scofield Reference Bible, no less, as she blew
the smoke across its pages and said, "Whooo! What do you think
Paul means by this?" I said to myself, "Friend, you can't come to
know Christ in here!"

I was never more wrong. I thought this lady's problem was her
smoke, but that wasn't her problem at all. It was her soul. And
most of us can't get beyond the smoke to the soul.

There is a marked difference between the church of A.D. 74 and
the church of A.D. 1974. The New Testament church was primarily
called to be a school, a training ground, a place for the equipment
of saints to do the work of the ministry. These saints were then to
go out and penetrate the society in which they found themselves
and to confront men and women with the Gospel of the Grace of
God.

Today we reverse those arrows. Instead of going out, we have
constituted the church as a soul-saving station, and if an individual
is going to come to know Christ, he must come to the church,
where a professional will present the Gospel to him. In effect we
put a sign up on the church that says, "Here we are, you lucky
sinners. Welcome!" And they stay away in droves.

Week after week the minister either preaches to a wilderness of
wood or evangelizes the evangelized.

The times demand the New Testament approach, with laymen
engaging in significant witness.

I love to share this story for two reasons. It records the confession of a seminary professor admitting he was wrong, which is
very refreshing. But even more important, it exposes a prevalent
attitude we Christians often show toward the non-Christian world.
We can be such a smug, stuffy bunch, drawing up our Pharisaical
skirts tight around us for fear of contamination. A home Bible

class ministry can really set us right about this problem, provide a great vehicle for evangelism, and illustrate in living lessons the ministry of the saints and the role of pastors.

The problem Howard Hendricks describes is not new; the Lord has always had to move his people through this "contamination" barrier. It's recorded early in the history of the church in Acts 10. Do you recall the story? I call it "The Tale of Two Hungry People." Here's a recap of the action in updated form.

Two Hungry People: The Italian and the Kosher Jew

There was this Italian army lieutenant who, in spite of his pagan background, knew how to pray—and even to share his pay with God's people. So God, responding to his hungry heart, made some rather elaborate arrangements to bring him to a personal knowledge of the Lord Jesus.

God sent him a messenger with instructions for him to seek a man called Peter who was staying by the seashore in Joppa. Cornelius obeyed immediately and sent his men to bring Peter to Caesarea.

Meanwhile, back at the seashore, Peter (the other hungry man) was waiting on the balcony for dinner to be prepared when God gave him a vision. (Whether Peter was asleep or conscious is hard to say.)

It was a very strange vision, especially to Peter, for he saw a sort of sheet come down out of heaven filled with all kinds of animals and reptiles and birds. A voice said to him, "Rise, Peter, kill and eat." But this kosher Jew replied, "No, Lord; for I have never eaten anything that is common or unclean." The voice again, "What God has cleansed, you must not call common." And three times this dialogue was repeated.

About this time Peter must have wondered what he ate for lunch that would give him such a nightmare. But right then Cornelius' men arrived from Caesarea and asked for Peter. If it had not been for the prompting of the Holy Spirit coinciding with the arrival of these men, Peter probably would have reached for the Alka-Seltzer and forgotten the whole thing.

But instead he asked, "Why are you here and what do you want?"

They explained their mission and invited Peter to go to the home of Cornelius to share his message with them. Peter invited them to stay the night and the next day they headed for Caesarea with Peter and some of his Christian friends.

A New Testament Home Bible Class

When they arrived at the house of Cornelius, what a sight greeted them! Cornelius had invited all his friends and relatives, and Peter found himself in a house full of people.

At first Cornelius, in his understandable pagan ignorance, tried to worship Peter, but Peter said, "Stand up, I'm just a man like you. And I'm sure you realize we Jews aren't supposed to fraternize with you pagans, but God showed me I'm not to consider you 'unclean' as I have all my life. Now, what do you want of me?"

A perfect introduction

So Cornelius told the story of his heavenly visitor and introduced Peter to his assembled guests with these words. "Now therefore we are all here present in the sight of God, to hear all you have been commanded by the Lord."

What a great introduction! We realize you are God's man with his message . . . now give it to us!

The next phrase is interesting: "And Peter opened his mouth . . ."

I should think so! Wouldn't you?

Good News—even for Italians!

Peter, the reluctant apostle, was finally turned loose with enough liberty to declare the Good News of Jesus Christ!

Here are a few snatches from his message. Read the rest for yourself in Acts 10:34 to 44:

"I see that God shows no partiality."
"You know the word—good news of peace by Jesus Christ."

"He is Lord of all!"

"They put him to death."

"But God raised him up and made him manifest."

"He is the one ordained by God to be judge of the living and the dead."

"Everyone who believes in him receives forgiveness of sins through his name."

That's about as straightforward a gospel presentation as you can get!

And, "While Peter was still saying this, the Holy Spirit fell on all who heard the word." He never finished his message! While Peter spoke they believed the Good News and entered into life!

I know lots of pastors and teachers who would love to have their messages end this way. No need for an invitation or ten verses of "Just As I Am"—just the ready response of hearts open to the Good News!

Here is a prime example of a New Testament home Bible class. Note the ingredients:

- A teacher—Peter
- A host—Cornelius
- A home opened to friends and relations through a hospitable, sharing heart
- The gospel presented
- Some prepared people with open hearts
- A clear response of faith

Looking deeper

But what are some of the deeper implications of this story? And what can we learn from it for our own use twenty centuries later?

The teacher—Peter

Look at Peter for a moment. He was not about to be moved from his "kosher" views. Those Gentiles were unclean! Did you notice the threefold repetition of the dialogue between Peter and the Lord? It must have gotten a little heavy the third time around the same sound track.

And how about Peter's classic "foot in mouth" statement: "No, Lord!" These words just won't go together. We can say "No" and we can say "Lord," but not "No, Lord." If he is truly Lord there's no way we can tell him no.

It's clear that Peter was thinking more of his empty stomach than about some heart-hungry Italian.

The host—Cornelius

How about that Italian? Here's a different story. Note:

•He was immediately responsive.
•He didn't delay or demur.
•He was eager to share God's message even before he heard it.
•He even invited his relatives! (Pretty good for a pagan Roman. Some of us don't do that well as Christians.)
•He gave the perfect introduction for a speaker: tell us what you've heard from God.
•He heard the gospel and believed *the first time* he understood about Jesus Christ in his saving work.

Behind the scenes

His story is really great. But what really put it all together? Did you notice?

It was God at work behind the scenes who really accomplished the results!

It was *he* who sent the two visions.

It was *he* who persuaded the reluctant apostle.

It was *he* who moved the heart of this pagan Roman to invite his friends.

It was *he* who sent the Holy Spirit upon them as they believed.

So what?

What can we learn, to apply to our twentieth century scene? Perhaps this:

•God can use a home as a beachhead for evangelism.

•There *are* hungry hearts around.

•We *do* need to shed our false views of Christian separationism.

•Worldlings are *not* unclean! They are ones for whom Christ died.

•We must stop saying "No, Lord" and begin to move out to them.

•We *can* go as "just a man" among men—without formal theological training or ecclesiastical sanction.

•We *must* tell the Good News about Jesus Christ, Lord of all!

•We can expect some to respond by trusting him and acknowledging his Lordship.

But perhaps most important of all:

•God is at work behind the scenes to set up the action.

But, too often, we Christians are slow to respond.

Is it possible that, as in this story, there are people out there in the world more ready to respond than we are to go and tell them the gospel?

I well remember one dear lady who discovered the joy of knowing Christ the very first time she heard the gospel presented in a home Bible study. God is still at work preparing hearts and seeking those who would worship Him!

More evidence

But before we leave the biblical scene for modern examples of the same kind of action, look with me at a couple more New Testament examples of a home Bible class ministry.

I always have to chuckle a bit to myself when I look at the example of Paul in Acts 18:5–8. Here we see the gospel message being rejected by the Jews in the synagogue, so Paul simply moved next door to the home of Titius Justus. And what happened there? Crispus, the ruler of the synagogue, became a Christian!

I like God's sense of humor. In effect he says, "You think you can thwart my program by rejecting my truth in your ecclesiastical setting? No problem—I'll just move next door." So a simple home setting becomes the place where Christ can "settle down and be at home" in believing hearts—even the heart of a Jewish religious leader!

Levi's class

Even earlier in the New Testament record we see the Lord Jesus in some of the same kind of action. In Mark 2:14 we see Jesus calling Levi, a publican (later called Matthew), to follow him. And the next verse records: ". . . as they sat at table in his [Levi's] house, many tax collectors and sinners were sitting with Jesus . . ." (Mark 2:15).

Here's a home Bible class scene with Jesus as the teacher! And what a likely bunch of candidates for salvation—tax collectors and sinners. It seems that Jesus sought out publicans quite often, for we see him calling Zacchaeus, "Come down out of that tree; I'm planning to stay with you" (Luke 19:1-7).

It Really Works!

Could we gather from this that perhaps the Lord would like to use our homes as a beachhead for evangelism, thru a simple Bible study approach?" I've seen it work so beautifully that examples come flooding into my mind. I'd love to share some with you.

There's the first home study I ever taught, more by accident than intent, but clearly by God's appointment. It began with a phone call from a friend who had recently become a Christian. He said, "Say, Bob, I have just begun to realize that I really don't know much about the Bible, and now that I'm a Christian I need to study it. Would you be able to come to our house and help us study the Scriptures?" Now, how can you say no to a request like that?

So we began, just the two families, to meet each week to study the Bible. The ensuing action, as I review it, was rather remarkable, and I can only explain it by the fact that God was at work behind the scenes in all of it. For just a few weeks later we counted thirty-two people in that living room scene. We didn't realize it, but we were in business.

The first response

The first one to receive Christ in that study was a young man of
Roman Catholic background who, out of the blue, went down to
a stationery store and bought birth announcement cards to send
to those of us who had been praying for him and sharing the
gospel with him. I still have the card. I kept it because I was so
impressed by the clear response to God's Word that it portrayed.
It reads like this:

> NAME: John Paul
> ARRIVED: October
> WEIGHT: Considerably less
> PARENTS: Our Father and His Son Jesus Christ

This, all without human pressure, but with human cooperation
in the program of God to reach hungry hearts with his truth. This
first one to acknowledge Christ in the home study was a good
friend of the host, and the first one he had invited to the study.

The next thing we knew, this new Christian (whom we'll call
John) showed up with nine people. Like Cornelius, he had invited his friends and relatives.

We learned later that John, a few days before he came to the
Bible study, had piled all his guns into his car after an argument
with his wife and roared off down the freeway at ninety miles per
hour. He told us that any cop who had stopped him would have
faced the muzzle of a loaded .38 caliber revolver.

Shortly after he became a Christian, John said one day to his
wife, "Dear, have you ever asked Christ into your life?" She
replied, "Why no, as a matter of fact I haven't." He said, "Why
don't you?" So she did!

Not long after that this young woman, with typical tenderness
and sensitivity, asked me, "Would you teach a class for just my
family? They're very shy folks, and I don't think they would come
to a public study." At the time I was already teaching several
times a week, in addition to a full-time engineering job, so I
said, "No, I'm sorry, but I just can't do it right now." She was
obviously disappointed, but didn't stop hoping and praying. A
few weeks later I had to tell her, "Let's start the class. The Lord
won't let me say no any longer."

And on—and on

We began a study of Romans from Phillips's "Letters to Young Churches" in their home, and the first night the hostess's aunt received Christ. A few weeks later when this woman's husband became a Christian, there began a flow of productive action that extended for the next several years.

The first year we had a class in this couple's home, they personally invited one hundred of their friends . . . and seventy of them came! Of that number at least fifteen or twenty (perhaps more) became Christians. It got so exciting and productive that we wondered what was wrong if someone didn't find the Lord each week.

Some Typical Action

We observed some remarkable responses in this home Bible study scene:

There was Emma, who was uninstructed but so concerned to get at the truth that she asked every question that popped into her head. She didn't care if it sounded dumb, she asked it anyway. And what an asset she was, for the very questions she phrased were in the minds of many others in the class who were too timid to ask them. Emma visibly changed (even in appearance) from week to week, as we confronted God's truth together—and it wasn't long before she was a Christian. She said one night, "I sure wish my husband could enjoy what I now know about the Lord, but he'll never get close enough to find out." Not more than a couple of months later he, too, was in Christ. He made the mistake of getting too close. He stopped to pick up his wife one night and responded to the host's gracious invitation to have a cup of coffee!

Mormons make good Christians

Then there was Rose, a lovely young woman of Mormon background, even related to some branch of the Brigham Young family. She found the joy and liberty of knowing Christ, and as a young Christian a few months old in the faith stood up against the local Mormon bishop with the testimony of a new life in Christ, standing on the Word of God. She confuted his attack so well that he got mad and said, "Stop quoting the Bible to me. That's a dead book!" She was ultimately accorded the honor of suffering for Christ's sake by being excommunicated from the Mormon church. All this she experienced as a young believer— and facing the hurt of not being understood by family and friends.

Another young Mormon woman sat in the Bible study until the sixth chapter of Romans, and suddenly burst into tears as I was teaching. I well remember the look I got from my wife as if to say, "What did you say to hurt this dear girl?" I wondered, too, because I find it easy to have "hoof-in-mouth" disease, and I thought perhaps I had offended her. My wife followed her out as she left the room and discovered the facts: she hadn't been offended at all, but as the Scripture unfolded to her understanding she suddenly realized that all the terrible burden laid on her by the legalistic Mormon system was totally unnecessary. She found through Romans 6 that Christ had borne all her sin and guilt and had set her free from slavery! Her tears were tears of joy, and really represented her confession of faith in Jesus Christ. She became, along with others I have mentioned, one of the most delightful open-hearted Christians I know.

Reaching men

You say, "You've told mostly about women. Do any men find the Lord in this home study scene?"

I'll say they do. One of the classic examples was a 240-pound ex-football-player man-about-town. He showed up at a Bible study at the invitation of a salesman friend. One of those extroverts who take charge in every situation, he went around greeting everybody as if he were the host instead of a recent arrival. Everyone knew he was around.

He sat down right under my nose and listened attentively as we studied Romans. (You've understood by now that we have found Romans to be a good landing place from which to expound the gospel.) As I recall, he made no comment the first week he came. And I said to myself, "We'll never see him back in this scene; he's too sophisticated and worldly to look for a second treatment with *this* material. But how wrong I was! He came the next week, made himself right at home, and asked the two best questions I've ever heard from a non-Christian.

I was reviewing the first several chapters of Romans, and in the process I used the word "sin" a number of times. (It's hard to avoid that word in Romans.) "Whaddya mean 'sin'? What's that?" He wasn't challenging the concept, he only wanted it defined. So I replied with several biblical definitions like: "To him that knows to do good and does it not—that is sin" (James 4:17) And, "Whatever does not proceed from faith is sin" (Rom. 14:23). (I wanted to be sure he had room to include himself in the target area.) With that he said, "Okay," and settled back to listen again.

A bit later I used the word *justified* (another word that's hard to avoid in Romans) and again he said, "Hey, hold it—whaddya mean 'justified'?"

This time I answered with a dictionary definition: "Webster says to be justified is to be declared blameless of sin on the grounds of Christ's righteousness, imputed by faith."

At that he got a bit wide-eyed and then seemed visibly to relax. We went on with the study, and when it concluded I thought, "I'd better move in on this guy tonight, for I don't expect him to show up a third time." (You're so right: I should have learned the first time not to sell God short—and I can still hear the Lord saying, "Oh, you of little faith.") Anyway, I sat down next to him and after an exchange of small talk I said, "Dave, do you know that my wife has been praying for you for over two years?" (We had met Dave about two years before he showed up at the Bible class, and my wife, Pearl, had been so struck by his fouled-up language that she began to pray that he might come to know the One whose name he tossed around so carelessly. To my shame, I had really not thought about him more than a few times in those two years.)

Dave's eyes misted up to the point of overflowing, and he replied, "Well, you can tell her that now she can stop."

This was his confession of faith in Christ—to say, in other words, "Her prayers have been answered." "Why don't *you* tell her?" I suggested. And he said, "I will."

He proceeded to seek Pearl out where she was serving coffee in the kitchen, clamped her in a great, big bear hug and gave her a resounding kiss. Pearl retreated in confusion, not knowing what it was all about until he explained, "I just want to say thanks—for caring and praying."

It turned out that Dave had visited church after church, had blown a small fortune "living it up" to try to find satisfaction, but apparently had to come to a simple little home Bible class to find out how to be justified by faith. I became "Old Dad" to him, and he often greeted me by planting a big kiss on my bald forehead—all to express his appreciation for one who would share the Good News of the gospel with a seemingly unreachable, sophisticated man-about-town.

Think this kind of action is worthwhile?

A nuclear physicist

A quite different situation was the case of a Stanford nuclear physicist. While working on the linear accelerator on the Stanford University campus in Palo Alto, Dr. John McIntyre somehow showed up at a home class I taught occasionally as part of the teaching team. He was a liberal education for me! Asking every question you could think of and some you wouldn't, he gave the typical scientific approach to the Bible and the Christian message. Usually you can expect the same ten to twenty questions from non-Christians, but John gave it a much more intensive and intelligent look than most. Every time we'd meet he would have another tough one, so much so that I began to duck around corners to avoid him (not really, but I began to *feel* like it). But he was never argumentative—always investigative. So, often I would say, "Jack, I don't know the answer to that one, but let's both check it out and compare notes next week." Invariably we would come up with explanations for the seeming discrepancy or problem which he would accept as satisfactory, and we would go on to the next question. Over a period of many months his investigation continued, until one day he was able to say, "My mind is satisfied that the Bible is reliable and trustworthy, not full of contradictions and errors as I'd been told." And yet he was still not a Christian. So he took one further step. He reasoned, "Having gone this far, if I'm being honest, I must respond to the demands the Bible makes on my will—not just my intellect."

About then he discovered the words of the Lord Jesus, "Behold, I stand at the door and knock; if anyone hears my voice and opens the door, I will come in to him and eat with him and he with me" (Rev. 3:20).

Here's a place I can check it out. "Lord, I'm opening the door. Now you *prove* to me that you've come in!" This was the scientist stepping out of his detached role as objective observer and putting *himself* in the experiment! And though his proposition may sound a bit presumptuous to some of us, I'm sure the Lord didn't mind a bit! All he really needs is a chance to prove his availability and confirm his presence in the life, and this is what John McIntyre proposed.* You know the outcome. Today this nuclear scientist is a committed Christian, enjoying his life in Christ.

All kinds of action

The life-changing ministry of the Lord at work in home Bible classes has reached all kinds of people from all kinds of backgrounds. There have been housewives, physicists, salesmen, teachers, milkmen, firemen, Christian Scientists, Mormons, Catholics, Jehovah's Witnesses, Episcopalians, plain American pagans, Humanists, liberals—you name it—from Ph.D's to beer bums, who have found joy of salvation in Jesus Christ through a simple home study of the Word of God.

If an Italian soldier (Cornelius) can make it in this scene, how about the rest of us?

---

* Dr. John McIntyre's testimony has been printed in *His* magazine as "A Physicist Believes." He has also written articles for *Christianity Today*. He was president of the American Scientific Affiliation in 1973.

What Happened to "Workers Together"?

How does all this fit into the church scene? Here's how: a pastor and his people can team up together like Peter and Cornelius did, only more so. The pastor can teach—not only teach the Scriptures in a home class, but also teach his people how to teach a home class. Remember? "Equipping the saints for a work of ministry" is the name of the game for pastors. The home of a Christian couple can provide the setting for the most exciting ministry you could ever imagine. The brief on "Friendship Evangelism Through Home Bible Classes" in Appendix I gives some guidelines.

The pastor's part

I remember a choice young doctor who teamed up with me on a home class. We would meet every Friday at 5:00 A.M. to review the class and discuss where we had won and where we had "missed it." He confided in me that on Mondays before the class he felt like selling the whole thing for a plug nickel and that it scared him more than taking his oral exams for his medical license. But on Tuesday after the class he wouldn't take a million for it. And the first one to find Christ in his class was a dear little Japanese girl who soon began sending a weekly air-letter exposition of Romans in Japanese script to her family in Tokyo!

Ready to try it?

Opportunity unlimited

We have seen all kinds of evangelistic Bible classes: small and large, in homes and industry, in America and Guatemala, informal and not-so-informal, in the supersophisticated culture of California and in the Oriental scene of inscrutable exteriors and face-saving. The opportunities abound for this ministry, for the human heart is the same everywhere—and the need for Jesus as Lord is all-pervasive.

Home classes

In our local scene we have had home classes as large as 300, if you're impressed by size. I can remember a class in the Atherton home of one of our elders where we counted 191 people. But a little circle of 15 or 20 in someone's living room is far better, in my estimation. But we don't quibble about numbers. We just minister to those whom God sends.

Industry classes

We have had classes in the business world, in such industrial complexes as Lockheed Missile & Space, Litton Industries, General Electric, and Pacific Telephone. One summer, using Moody *Sermons From Science* films in both home and industrial settings, together with testimony and commentary by scientific-minded Christian men, we figured out we reached about seven thousand men and women with the message of God's grace in just ten weeks. One of our men in the telephone company has teamed up with other Christians in the company to make studies available and get them announced in the company paper. This action has even spread from the San Francisco office to the Fresno area. See their study format in Appendix J. It's a good one.

The program was so well received at Lockheed that each week it moved to larger rooms until Lockheed began to have trouble getting the use of its own conference rooms. We may have set back the program for outer space in favor of God's plans for inner space!

Then, after the first series of film showings, the Lockheed management received complaints from the shop stewards—not because the films were being shown, but because the hourly employees (who only had a half-hour for lunch) didn't get to see them! So a group of Christians at Lockheed set up a second series of films to be shown during the lunch hour—in the cafeteria!

In foreign lands

I have personally taught a Bible class in the home of the mayor of Guatemala City, with the U.S. ambassador, some U. N. delegates and most of the city council in attendance. And, believe it or not, we had a pointed, lively discussion of the Christian message through an interpreter. The U.S. ambassador, Gordon Mains, a Christian, said to me after the class, "This is the first time I've ever been 'bait' for a Bible class." He realized that if he were there, all the nationals would want to attend, too. Ambassador Mains was later tragically assassinated by radical elements in that country.

The following week in Guatemala I taught a Bible class in an Episcopalian priest's home with mostly lawyers attending. And I shall never forget the city secretary, Mario Guerra, who was very kind to me personally. He sort of attached himself to me in one of those relationships only the Lord can create. After quizzing me until midnight at the class, he wrote a letter in Spanish to me at home, telling me that he considered me his spiritual counselor. What amazing things the Lord can do, even with some of the world's important people through a country boy from California.

But the best home study I had in Guatemala was in the Christian warmth of the home of a delightful couple, Juan Jose Rodas and his wife, Ketty. Here was the relaxed, open and participative kind of scene I look for as ideal. We considered the claims of Christ in John's Gospel, in a realistic confrontation of the Son of God. And I shall never forget the loving Latin *abrazo* of little Juan as his arms reached to surround this big, old "Norte-Americano" in a parting expression of thanks for sharing God's good things.

The reality of armed political conflict, with people being killed just a few blocks away from Judge Rodas's home, was a pointed contrast to the gracious, redemptive climate of that living room scene focused around the One who is our peace, as the *Prince of Peace*.

In another land and culture, a missionary friend of mine in Japan adapted the idea of a film ministry through the church to the home environment. He calls it "Family-size Evangelism." The viability of this plan is being demonstrated as well suited to the Japanese culture. After all, it began in an Oriental culture. Why should it not work there?

Variations on a theme

In my view, variations on the theme of evangelistic Bible studies are endless: there are sharing-type studies, discussion group approaches, downtown noontime studies in restaurants or executive clubs—you name it. A man I know even began a Saturday morning study in his office with his ten best customers. He asked them to read the book of Proverbs and try to find a statement to include on their business cards.

Some Obvious Advantages

A home Bible class ministry offers some considerable advantages over most other forms of evangelism. Here are some of them.

- •People will come to a home to study the Bible. It is a keen opportunity for honestly inquiring folks to get answers to some of their long-standing questions.
- •There are no financing problems. As long as the host can keep making payments on his mortgage there's a place to meet. The participating Christians can share the costs of coffee and cookies. So we can present the gospel without charge or financial appeal.
- •We can just present Jesus as Lord, since we have nothing to join and thus no road blocks to hinder open, honest consideration of the gospel. Barriers topple when our non-Christian friends discover this.
- •It employs the body of Christ in Christian cooperation and thus relieves pastors of the impossible job of trying to reach the whole world by themselves.
- •There is built-in follow-up, first through Christian friendship to the ones we invite, but also by the continuity of teaching through the Scriptures.
- •We reach the right audience, our own friends and neighbors, by taking the message of Christ to them.
- •It gets Christians charged up about their life and ministry, because it's exciting to see God at work changing lives. Also, they get opportunity to interact with real-life problems and

questions and learn how to meet them. It's pretty hard to be bored in this atmosphere.

•It combines zeal and knowledge. The new-found love for Christ and the joy of life in him so beautifully seen in new Christians teams up with the maturity and knowledge of the older ones. Maximum advantage accrues to the non-Christian contacts of both to understand the truth of God.

•Christ is preached to those whose eternal destiny is at stake, and some will believe! Unfortunately not all will receive Christ, but all who come will have a clearer understanding of the proposition presented in the gospel. It's up to them to say yes or no to Christ, as they will. But many say yes! Perhaps some are just waiting for our approach to them right now (like Cornelius).

As God's people, beginning with pastors, perhaps we should get serious about using this exciting vehicle for reaching our lost friends and neighbors through some form of evangelistic Bible studies. I'm sure the Lord has ways to show you that we've never learned! How about it?

PAINT IT!

CHAPTER SEVEN

MOTIVATING MEN

An old army game that is played equally well outside the military goes something like this. In the never-ending shuffle of paper work and material the idea is, "Keep it moving!" Never get caught with the stuff on your desk. And, "If you can't move it, paint it!"

Somehow this same philosophy has invaded our thinking in the church. Moving men to action, the kind of action God wants, is difficult—so we paint them into the scene, usually sitting in the pews.

Moving Men to Action

Why is it so hard to move people to action? There are any number of reasons. Let's look at a few:

"I don't know what I could contribute, except my ignorance. I wouldn't know what to do."

"Oh, I couldn't do that! I've never done anything like that before."

Or, "I just serve the Lord in my own quiet, humble way, but I'd never be able to handle that kind of job. That's too much for me!"

So our first motivational problem is how to change "Mission Impossible" to "Mission Possible." We all need to know the resources from which we operate—and that they are adequate.

Moving Moses—and me

God has this problem with each of us, so it's not new to him. An early account of the way he motivates is found in his conversation with Moses recorded in Exodus 3:7–4:14. An up-dated version of this account might sound something like this:

"I've got a job for you, Moses. I want you to go to the king of Egypt and tell him you're going to take all his Hebrew slaves out of his country." (The modern equivalent of this would be to announce to the Russian government that you intend to set free all their captive peoples, including those in Hungary and Czechoslovakia.)

"Who, me? Who am I to tackle this kind of suicide mission?" Moses' reply was not surprising.

"But I will be with you," the Lord answered.

It would seem that this should make a difference—that what God proposes to do he can accomplish, through any instrument. But Moses was not convinced. So he brought out his next objection. "Who are you? If I go to the children of Israel and tell them what you're proposing, they'll say, 'Says who? Who gave you this wild-eyed idea?' What can I say then?"

At this point in his life, even after some thirty-five years at God's Desert Training Camp in Midian, Moses still didn't know his God. (Do you suppose we share his problem?)

So God, in simple, regal terms, replied, "*I am who I am.*"

The force of these words hardly penetrates the English language. While in English it sounds as if God is saying, "It's none

of your business," it is really a play on the verb *to be*, and conveys
the idea that God is the eternally self-existent One with no
beginning; the One who has always been around and is always
here. "Tell them that I AM sent you." Following this declaration,
God stated in clear terms what he intended to do through Moses.

Moses still objected. (How like us!) "But look, they'll never
believe me," he said.

"What do you have in your hand?"

"A rod."

"Throw it on the ground." It became a snake. And Moses ran!
"Come on back. Don't be afraid. Pick up the snake by its tail."

"By its tail! That's no way to handle a poisonous reptile! You
must be kidding!"

"Come on now—do what I tell you." (Did God ever tell you
to do something that seemed totally unreasonable? He usually
does. But think it through. If we could figure out everything,
how would he stretch our faith? His thinking and acting would
be pretty puny if it were limited to what we can understand!)

So Moses did it! To his credit, he began to be a man of faith
at last. And the snake became a rod again, to be from that time
on the symbol of the authority of faith.

Well, at this point it looked as if Moses had the idea, but obviously the life of faith is not learned in one easy lesson. So he
objected again. "But, Lord, I can't talk." Have you ever noticed
how eloquent we can be, attempting to explain that we can't talk?

But God, still patiently reasoning, replied, "Who made man's
mouth? Is it not I, the Lord? Now, go ahead; I will be with your
mouth and teach you what to say." (What an offer! Yet it's the
same idea we get in the New Testament in, "Nevertheless I live,
yet not I, *but Christ lives in me*" (Gal. 2:20) and ". . . we have
this treasure in earthen vessels, to show that the transcendent
power belongs to God and not to us" (2 Cor. 4:7).

But Moses declined the offer. "Lord, send someone else."

At this, God got mad!

Do you see why? Up to that point Moses had said, "Lord, I'm
inadequate, I can't do it." But now the implication is "And I
don't believe you can do it either." No wonder God was angry!
But how often do *we* do this same thing? Oh, I know we can

say, "I wish God spoke to me that plainly; then I'd do what he says." Certainly there is *some* validity to that argument, because sometimes we honestly don't know. But we need not remain in ignorance; God has promised to give wisdom to anyone who asks (James 1:5-8). Actually there's no excuse for either Moses or us, since *unbelief* is the real problem in either case. It isn't that we dont' know (or can't find out) what God wants!

What do we have in our hands but a whole book full of instructions on what God wants of us and *commands* to be obeyed, even *pleadings* to enlist our cooperation. God has provided all the encouragement our hearts could desire. His word to us is, "As I was with Moses—so I am with you."

AS I WAS . . . SO I AM

"As I was with Moses, so I am with thee."
Wondrous words of promise for the untried road;
Think, my soul, Who said them—God, Almighty God!
Words of strong assurance; words which bring heart-rest:
With such Presence with me can I be unblest?
"As I was with Moses so I am with thee"—
Statement more than promise, great with certainty;
Unknown though the future, untried though the way,
With His presence by me shall I go astray?
"As I was with Moses"—(meekest man on earth,
Yet whose meekness made him man of priceless worth)—
"So I am with thee"—thus, quite undismayed,
We may journey with Him—calm and unafraid.
"As I was with Moses—"! So, this word sublime,
Can afford rich comfort—in this later time;
We who own His PARDON may His PRESENCE know,
Drawing on His mighty POWER daily here below.

J. Danson Smith

Facing the facts

Some strong motivating principles can be drawn from this story:

84 WHEN ALL ELSE FAILS . . .

1. We have adequate resources in our indwelling Lord. Every demand he makes on us he knows can only find its supply in him! We can know it, too. "He who calls us is faithful, and he will do it" (1 Thess. 5:14).

2. We can trust the Lord to do what he says he will do.

3. God does call us to a "Mission Impossible" to show us that he can "do far more than we can ask or even think—according to his power at work in us" (Eph. 3:20). He is the God of the impossible, but with God "the impossible takes a little longer" because we are so slow to believe him.

How can we move men to action? The same way God moves us to action—by showing them from the Scripture what God wants and then appealing to them to believe it, in specific terms, on a personal level.

Turning Facts into Acts

In practice, this involves some approaches that dignify God's appeal.

1. *Make a personal, direct appeal, man to man,* instead of relying on the "volunteer" system. (I recall telling one young man that I believed he had the gift of teaching and I would like to help him develop the use of it. His eyes filled with tears at the thought that someone would be that concerned about his life and ministry.)

2. *Convey the sense of value that God sets forth* in saying that 'the head cannot say to the foot, I have no need of you" (1 Cor. 12:21). Everyone has a valued place in the body, and it's God who says so! We need to give every member a sense of vital participation in the action of the body.

3. *Give continuing expressions of encouragement and appreciation.* No one wants to be treated like a piece of furniture! Love does not take people for granted.

4. *Take the initiative to be available to people.* Let them share your ministry. Take them with you. Use them in the pulpit. Give them exploratory opportunities. Help them discover their gifts.

5. *Give ample training opportunities.* Provide classes of instruction for every phase of life and ministry. Use the understudy

approach and have an associate participating with you in teaching, evangelism, visiting, and other ministry.

6. *Don't be afraid to let others evaluate your performance.* Use "critique" method to show them where they fail and how to do it better, but start by being vulnerable yourself.

7. *Periodically review personnel.* Consciously think through who is around and not functioning. Where does he or she fit in the body? What are their gifts and ministries? Publicize ministry opportunities to open the door for participation and exploration.

8. *Maintain a continuing thread of teaching to encourage a walk of faith.* This is the basis upon which people enter into a place of ministry. Apart from faith they'll never start!

9. *Back up those who enter into a place of ministry. Don't desert them!* A good shepherd doesn't walk off and leave his flock. Stay with them especially when they fail. Even then, Jesus is still victor! We can learn the greatest lessons from our failures. The Apostle Paul discovered this in his hour of great discouragement and recorded: "But thanks be to God, who in Christ always leads us in triumph . . ." (2 Cor. 2:14).

Digging deeper

What motivates men?

It is not oversimplifying to say that ordinarily men are moved to action by the prospect of gaining something of value to them.

Why do so many people go for the "sure fling" of Las Vegas? Obviously they think they might hit the jackpot and take home a pocketful of cash. They may know the mathematical probabilities are all against them, and they certainly understand that the high-priced entertainers, fancy casinos, and lavish food and drink are not provided to make it pleasant while customers get rich at the expense of the house. But they always think they can beat the odds and break the bank.

I have a friend who blew $6800 in one gambling spree and has spent years trying to recover financially. Why did he do it? He was motivated by the prospect of gaining something he wanted —more money.

It is a sad situation in industry today that men are overpaid and undermotivated. Money-motivation is all that many see in their jobs, so they and their unions keep grabbing for higher pay and shorter work-weeks, usually not knowing how to make proper use of either the money or the leisure time they gain.

Our own experience could multiply examples of the non-existent or short-lived gains promised by worldly motivation. The Christian has it all over the world in this department. Just think, we can present the prospect of the greatest gain men's hearts could desire—the genuine fulfillment and eternal value of our personal partnership with Christ in his great redemptive work! Here is motivation that counts. Why don't we present it more clearly and attractively? Too often the world and the flesh win out with their shoddy and dead-end motivation, even over Christians.

Mere Christianity—or Discipleship?

Could it be we have missed the point of our Lord's chief moti-vating appeal? Often the Great Commission passage in Matthew 28 has been used as a charge to evangelize the world. Certainly this is valid, but a careful study of these verses reveals that evangelism is *not* its main thrust. A closer look reveals that *making disciples* is to be our aim. Evangelizing is only part of the process of discipling. Let's examine the words in detail.

And Jesus came and said to them, "All authority in heaven and on earth has been given to me. Go therefore and *make disciples* of all nations, *baptizing* them in the name of the Father and of the Son and of the Holy Spirit, *teaching* them to observe all that I have commanded you; and lo, I am with you always, to the close of the age" (Matt. 28:18–20).

The structure of these verses is centered in the verb forms: *go, make disciples, baptizing* and *teaching*. But only one of these is a finite verb (or main verb) while the other three are participles, or participating verb forms, modifying and explaining the main verb action.

Literally, it says, "Going, *make disciples*, baptizing and teach-ing." The emphasis is clearly to *make disciples*. The first word,

"Go", is not a command, as our English translations would make it, but rather says, "going" (in effect—"I assume you're on your way").

The second participle, *baptizing*, needs some clarification of its meaning. It can refer to the ritual act of water baptism, but here it has far deeper import than mere ritual observance. All the other verb forms convey *reality*, not ritual, so it is logical to assume that this verb should do no less, in such an important context. The functional use of this word in Greek, as distinct from its ritual significance, means *to introduce into a new relationship* —in this case, the new relationship of having the resources of the Godhead made available.

The word *name* also requires some added understanding: ". . . in the *name* of the Father and of the Son and of the Holy Spirit" means "into the *resources* of the Father, Son and Spirit." This is based on the idea that a person's name represents all that he is and has. "Open in the name of the law!" implies all the authority and resources of the government behind it.

Putting the passage all together, we would read it this way: ". . . All authority in heaven and on earth has been given to me; going therefore, *make disciples* of all nations, introducing them into all the resources of the Father and the Son and the Holy Spirit, teaching them to observe all that I have commanded you; and lo, I am with you always, to the close of the age.

The Great Commission, Revised Version

The one command is to *make disciples*, and the emphasis is on our Lord's available resources from which to operate. Making disciples involves *going, introducing into the total resources of the Godhead* and *teaching* the truth of God. Thus, the Great Commission is far more than just evangelizing; it involves showing people the total resources available to them in the Godhead through teaching them the Word of God. A disciple is basically a "learner," one who has put himself under the discipline of the Lord Jesus and is willingly subject to all he commands. What he is to learn is how to use the total resources now made available to him since he is in Christ.

This brings into focus the final motivating factor. *We must lead men to be disciples of Christ, responsive to his leadership—allowing him to be Lord.* Thus, we should enlist without pressure, allowing men freedom to respond to the Lord Jesus, not just to us. We can thus help them to seek the clear call of God to their avenue of service for him. Our place and privilege is to encourage them to explore, expose them to opportunities of service, then to let them observe the results and respond to the Lord from their own hearts. It is amazing what happens when we do this. The Lord *does* call them and confirm his appointed sphere of service for them. And becoming *his* disciples, they learn to draw on the adequate spiritual capital of a totally sufficient God.

A SERVANT ATTITUDE

CHAPTER EIGHT

KINKS IN THE LINKS

But what about some of the problem areas? For instance—

How about Deacons?

Some concepts in the Bible and the words which describe them need to be rescued from man-made distortions which, through the accretions of the centuries, have completely or seriously clouded their meaning. The word *deacon* (and the concepts which surround its usage in ecclesiastical circles) is one of those words.

In order to gain renewed perspective on such a word we must review its use in the total context of the Bible, endeavoring at the same time to cast off our ingrained preconceptions, to arrive at a wholly biblical understanding of the word and its use.

We propose to do this with the word *deacon* and then relate it to the life of the church, hopefully as God intends us to understand it.

Deacon is a loan word which we have borrowed from the Greeks. In the Greek New Testament it takes three forms:

(1) *diakonos,* from which we get *deacon.*

(2) *diakonia,* usually translated *service* or *ministry.*

(3) *diakoneo, to serve* or *to minister,* the verb form.

We would like to trace the meaning of this word through its use in secular Greek, the changes in meaning effected by Jewish thought, and finally the meaning derived from its use by the Lord Jesus and throughout the New Testament. We will refer to the word *diakonia* as representing the other forms as well for the sake of brevity of expression, so keep in mind that *diakonia* is the *service; diakonos* is *the one who serves;* and *diakoneo* is *the act of serving.*

Diakonia in Secular Greek

In secular usage, *diakonia* has its origin in the idea *to wait at table,* but it broadened from this to the idea of providing or caring for the needs of another. From there it became the service of love rendered to another on a personal basis. Lest we read into this definition too much of our current Christian thinking, we need to add that in the Greek mind this was not a very worthy of worthwhile activity—more demeaning than dignifying.

The Jewish view

Jewish thought patterns, for obvious reasons, considered service of this sort not unworthy or lacking in dignity, but thought it rather a work of merit before God, not really an unselfish sacrifice for another. So in the Jewish view it became acceptable to serve only those who were worthy. The unworthy and despised were not to be recipients of their service, as evidently portrayed in our Lord's story of the Good Samaritan (Luke 10:29–37).

"Service" in the words of Jesus

It took the ministry of the Lord Jesus in the New Testament record to elevate *diakonia* to its full expressiveness. By his life and in his teaching he elevated this word above its usage in both Greek and Hebrew thought patterns.

Jesus completely reversed the existing order when he said: "Blessed are those servants whom the master finds awake when he comes, truly, I say to you, he will gird himself and have them sit at table, and he will come and serve [*diakoneo*] them" (Luke 12:37).

Here the picture is that of *the master serving the slaves!*

He portrayed the *normal* order of things when he asked: "Will any one of you, who has a servant plowing or keeping sheep, say to him when he has come in from the field, 'Come at once and sit down at the table'? Will he not rather say to him, 'Prepare supper for me, and gird yourself and serve [*diakoneo*] me, till I eat and drink; and afterward you shall eat and drink'?" (Luke 17:7–8). Then he made it clear that he himself came to serve, by these words: "For which is the greater, one who sits at the table or one who serves [*diakoneo*]? Is it not the one who sits at table? But I am among you as *one who serves* [*diakoneo*]" (Luke 22:27).

And our Lord supremely demonstrated his servant attitude in John 13 when he took the slave's place and washed his disciples' feet. The word *diakonia* is not in this text, but the idea that it conveys is clearly portrayed in the action of this scene. Our Lord further expanded and dignified the idea of serving by linking it with the ultimate service of giving his life on our behalf in the service rendered at the cross: ". . . even as the Son of Man came not to be served [*diakoneo*] but to serve [*diakoneo*], and to give his life a ransom for many" (Matt. 20:28).

The meaning of *diakonia* is further widened by our Lord to encompass a wide spectrum of services such as giving food and drink, providing shelter, providing clothes, visiting the sick and imprisoned (Matt. 25:42–44). There, too, the Lord Jesus brought in another element of loving service rendered to another person —the idea that for his people service given to men was also service rendered to him: ". . . Truly, I say to you, as you did it to the least of these my brethren, you did it to me" (Matt. 25:40). In all of this we see that *diakonia* comes to mean the full range of expressions of active Christian love to one's neighbor. And since the Lord Jesus was himself the living example of this attitude it also became the hallmark of discipleship to him: "By this all men will know that you are my disciples, if you have love for one another" (John 13:35). He makes it clear in the context of this verse that love finds its expression in acts of loving service to one another.

Perhaps the capstone of our Lord's words on this subject are these: ". . . You know that those who are supposed to rule over the Gentiles lord it over them, and their great men exercise authority over them. *But it shall not be so among you; but whoever would be great among you must be your servant [diakonos], and whoever would be first among you must be slave of all"* (Mark 10:43).

And these: "Truly, truly I say to you, unless a grain of wheat falls into the earth and dies, it remains alone; but if it dies, it bears much fruit. He who loves his life loses it, and he who hates his life in this world will keep it for eternal life. If anyone *serves [diakoneo]* me, he must follow me; and where I am, there shall my *servant [diakonos]* be also; if anyone *serves [diakoneo]* me, the Father will honor him" (John 12:24–26).

Here we see service linked to dying, the sacrifice of one's own desires for the sake of another's well being. The Christian's service is clearly to parallel the service rendered by his Lord.

Diakonia *in the New Testament*

The scope of this word in the New Testament is broad and inclusive. It covers:

- •Timothy and Erastus as assistants in preaching the gospel (Acts 19:22).
- •Onesiphorus in his service to Paul at Ephesus (2 Tim. 1:16–18).

•The apostles' service to the church (2 Cor. 3:3).
•The Old Testament prophets' service to the church (1 Pet. 1:10–12).
•Paul ministering to the needs of the saints at Jerusalem (2 Cor. 8:19 and Romans 15:31).
•Ministry of the saints in general (Eph. 4:11, Heb. 6:10).
•The household of Stephanas devoting themselves to the service of the saints (1 Cor. 16:15).
•The ministry of angels (Heb. 1:14, Mark 1:13).

Service is coupled with other words to describe a particular form of ministry:

•Preaching the gospel as a ministry of the Word, in which the preacher is the one who serves up the Bread of Life (2 Tim. 4:5, Acts 6:4).
•This is also called a ministry of reconciliation (2 Cor. 5:18).
•All self-effort to keep the law is called a ministry of death and condemnation (2 Cor. 3:7–9).
•While in the same passage, by contrast, the life of faith is characterized as a ministry of the Spirit and a ministry of righteousness (2 Cor. 3:7–9).

Also, one can be:

a servant of Satan (2 Cor. 11:14–15),
or of God (2 Cor. 6:3, 1 Thess. 3:1–3),
of Christ (1 Tim. 4:6),
of the gospel (2 Cor. 11:23),
of a new covenant (2 Cor. 3:6),
of the church (Col 1:25).

Deacons as officials

It is commonly supposed that there is in the church the "office" of deacon in addition to, or as opposed to the general functioning of a Christian in a service or ministry described up to this point in our study. This view has perhaps been encouraged and implanted by the King James translation which uses the term "office" in translating 1 Timothy 3:13. "For they that have used the *office* of a deacon well purchase for themselves a good degree . . ." (AV).

Let's examine the validity of this idea. A literal translation of this verse would not contain the word *office*, but would read: "For the ones having served well acquire for themselves a good standing and much boldness in the faith. . . ." We need not strain too hard at the "office" idea from this text. It isn't actually there.

Deacons and bishops

In Philippians 1:1, the deacons are linked with the bishops (or overseers) which could lead us to believe that there were two kinds or groups of officials in the church. This may be so, but we could argue with equal weight that the apostle is here covering a spectrum of saints in this address. He could be saying, ". . . to *all* the saints in Christ Jesus who are at Philippi, with the overseers and household servants . . ." (Phil. 1:1). There is no real warrant for thinking Paul is addressing two groups of officials, even though we have been conditioned to think this way.

On the other side, however, there seems to be some sense in which deacons are representatives of a local church, for they are addressed with the bishops when the Apostle sets forth the requirements for these men in 1 Timothy 3:1–13 (though Titus 1:5–9 and 1 Peter 5:1–4 omit any mention of deacons in reviewing the requirements of the bishops).

We could infer from this reference to God's qualifications for deacons in 1 Timothy that they were in a recognized place of authority along with the bishops, but this is nowhere actually taught. We could equally well decide that all we really know is that deacons, as household servants, were called upon to live out a godly quality of life. This could be because they are to portray before men the same character as the One who came as a servant —the one whom Isaiah prophetically called "servant" in 52:13, the Lord Jesus.

It appears we cannot arbitrarily conclude that there was an "office" of deacon. Rather it seems more in keeping with the biblical evidence to conclude that deacons were and are those called of God to fulfill a special ministry in the household of God, of value to the whole body of believers and acting as representatives of the local church, thus the specifications in 1 Timothy.

But how about Acts 6?

The sixth chapter of Acts sheds a great deal of light on the appointment and function of deacons in the early church. And though *diakonos* is not used to identify those appointed in the scene, *diakonia* and *diakoneo* are used in Acts 6:1–2 of the ministry they performed, specifically here as *to serve tables*. To review the action, you may recall that there was a problem regarding the distribution of food between the Hellenists (or Greek-speaking) and Jewish widows, so the church leaders (in this case the apostles) called a meeting of the church to solve the problem. Their approach was direct and to the point: "We have a problem; we cannot be pulled away from the priority matter of the study and preaching of God's word to 'wait on tables,' so we want to delegate this job. You choose seven men from your number to handle it. But they must fit these specifications: (1) "They must be men of good repute, (2) men filled with the Spirit, (3) and full of wisdom" (Acts 6:3).

Wise leaders

It is apparent that they acted in God-given wisdom, since this was no simple problem: there were racial and religious implications, and the fight was between two groups of women!

The men chosen had to satisfy the people involved; thus the church was to select them. They had to be men whose fairness was well known, hence "men of good reputation." They needed the wisdom that God alone can provide, to handle this delicate matter between believers, so they must be "full of the Spirit and of wisdom." Thus we see that the apostles were wise in their stipulation of the method of handling and the qualifications of the deacons. But notice, too, the rest of their handling: "Pick out seven men . . . whom we may appoint to this duty" (Acts 6:3).

The seven deacons were (1) picked by the congregation, and (2) appointed by the apostles—an interesting combination of congregational action and apostolic oversight. Note, however, that the apostles reserved to themselves the appointive role. This is consistent with their spiritual leadership responsibility and overseeing ministry to the church. This responsible action was confirmed when "these [deacons] they set before the apostles, and they prayed and laid their hands on them" (Acts 6:6), the expression of identification and approval.

Deacons—but not always

One more observation: in Acts 7, Stephen, one of the men appointed, is seen preaching his marvelous sermon to the Jewish council. And in Acts 8 we see Philip, also one of the seven, evangelizing a Samaritan city, so it seems clear that they were not exercising the "office" of deacon in the Jerusalem church as permanent officials. Their appointment we take as performing a loving service in solving a problem in the assembly.

Can We Follow?

We suggest that the twentieth-century church should follow this example: Allow the assembly to choose its own leadership for areas of ministry, but consistent with the scriptural and spiritual qualifications set forth by the church leaders (apostles in the early beginning, then elders), and the appointments to be made and backing confirmed by the leaders, as responsible before God for the spiritual overseeing of the local body. In practice this approach would seem to apply to the selection of committees, leaders of men's and women's fellowship groups, etc. The duration of service can be long or short, depending on the demands of the task and extent of need.

Sure, there are problems

There are undoubtedly problems attendant with this procedure, but given the genuine exercise of the lordship of Christ and the love of the brethren in each case, they should not be insurmountable. Where the situation parallels Acts 6, at least, this solution should be applied, as it appears to have solved the problem and restored harmony in this instance.

This example is an explicit use of the word *diakonia* to mean "waiting on tables" and as "a service of love rendered to another person." Here, too, deacons were to be godly men, ministering in the name of Christ and exemplifying the character of Christ, as representatives of the local body.

So—

Our conclusion is that the Scriptures do not teach that there is a governing function or "office" of deacon, or that a board of deacons is to govern the church, but that deacons are many and varied in the local church scene, as servants ministering out of love to meet the needs of the local body. There do seem to be two categories, however: (1) the general broad-based ministry of household servants and (2) deacons appointed as representatives of the local body of believers. Also, it seems apparent that some governing boards being called deacons are really overseers or guardians in actual function.

A beautiful example of the general, grass-roots functioning of a deacon came to my attention recently. A young Christian girl gave a dinner for a newly married couple who were moving away. She invited about twenty-five of their friends to share a gracious evening around the table where she herself served a lovely full-course dinner for their enjoyment. The evening ended for her in washing dishes until 2:30 A.M. As I saw her literally "waiting on table" and expressing in this whole occasion "a loving service to Christian friends" whom she loved, it said one word to me— *diakonia*—and it was a joy to see! Romans 16:1 records a first-century ministry of this sort: "I commend to you our sister Phoebe, a deaconess of the church at Cenchreae, that you may receive her in the Lord as befits the saints, and help her in whatever she may require from you, for she has been a helper of many and of myself as well."

The gift of service

How does the gift of service or administration as listed among the spiritual gifts in Romans 12:7 fit into our understanding of *diakonia?* This is not hard to see if we recall that spiritual gifts are given for the building up of the body as a special measure, over and above the lowest-common-denominator level of Christian life and expression. For instance, every Christian has faith, for this is the way he *became* a Christian, by grace through faith. But every Christian does not have the *gift* of faith, which is evidently a greater measure of the same quality. Again, every Christian is expected to give, as an expression of Christian love, but every Christian does not have the *gift* of giving or making contributions. Barnabas is a classic example of a Christian with the gift of exhortation—so much so that Barnabas, meaning "son of encouragement," was actually his nickname.

So it is with the gift of service. Those who have this gift are to be an example and encouragement to the rest to go and do likewise, since they represent the One who came to serve.

To sum up

We have reviewed many of the uses of *diakonos, diakonia,* and *diakoneo*—enough, we trust, to get the flavor of this word and what it represents in terms of "deacons" in the church. Our conclusion is that there are to be a multitude of deacons and deaconesses expressing their life in the Lord Jesus through varied avenues of loving service. In essence these words capture the very spirit of our Lord Jesus in his servant character. I cannot help reflecting where we would be if He were not inclined to show this wonderful attitude of heart. And what the church (and the world) would be like without the real "deacons" and "deaconesses" with their acts of loving care.

But God reaffirms this calling to us through the apostle:

> So if there is any encouragement in Christ, any incentive of love, any participation in the Spirit, any affection and sympathy, complete my joy by being of the same mind, having the same love,

being in full accord and of one mind. Do nothing from selfishness or conceit, but in humility count others better than yourselves. Let each of you look not only to his own interests, but also to the interests of others. Have this mind among yourselves, which you have in Christ Jesus, who, though he was in the form of God, did not count equality with God a thing to be grasped, but emptied himself, taking the form of a *servant*, being born in the likeness of men. And being found in human form he humbled himself and became obedient unto death, even death on a cross" (Phil. 2:1–8).

From "being in the form of God" to "taking the form of a servant" seems to us a tremendous downward step of condescension, but to the Son of God it was the natural expression of his character, just being as he is. This comes out in bold relief from the word in the Greek text translated "form." In "taking the *form* of a servant" the word is *morphe*, which means the expression of the true inner nature. So the essential inner nature of the Lord Jesus is that of a *servant*. By contrast, "being found in human *form*" uses a Greek word that signifies a form which was *not* his natural or normal mode of being.

That our Lord is this way shouldn't surprise us, for God is love (1 John 4:8), and love delights to serve. And so it is (or should be) with deacons, God's gift to the church as household servants, doing all those menial (but not demeaning) chores around the house out of love and as unto the Lord.*

Assessing Needs

Lack of sensitivity to needs is an area of frequent administrative failure. Long-standing traditional boundaries very often restrict our freedom to think under the direction of the Spirit of God.

My past experience in the engineering field taught me a significant lesson on this subject. In confronting design problems I frequently found myself completely hemmed in by my thought processes. But when I freed myself from the built-in conditions

---

* Note: A complete listing of the usage of *diakonos*, *diakonia*, and *diakoneo* for further study is set forth in Appendix D.

I had so easily assumed, invariably I found ideas and answers
which were not previously in my field of vision.

If we need this freedom in designing a machine, consider how
much more important it is in thinking through the total church
program and every facet of ministry—under the Lord's direction!
He is never lacking in creative imagination. And if we are
honestly willing to evaluate our programs, weighing them against
observed needs among our people, without feeling threatened
that some pet project might be scuttled, then we are free to hear
the Lord's answer to our problem.

On Quiet Commitals

Sometimes, as Howard Hendricks says, "We just need a quiet
committal." In other words, when a program is dead already,
what we need to do is bury it! After saying a fond farewell and
offering a prayer of thanks for former days of usefulness and
vitality, we can then go on to that current expression of life
which the Lord has in mind for us.

This is not easy. Our attachments and those of our people go
deeper than we realize. In one church I know that is trying to
think through a better answer to the Christian education of our
children than the Sunday school, the anguished reactions are
deep. One would think that the Sunday school movement began
in the first century, and that the Apostle Paul was the first
Sunday school superintendent.

Admittedly, we need to be wary of going off on wild ideas just
for the sake of trying something new. And certainly we must have
something better to offer before we scrap existing vehicles. But
in Christian maturity we need to shake off whatever inhibiting
factors keep us from seeing and implementing God's new plan of
action, if he has one for us.

Facing Failure

We need, also, to be willing to fail in some of our attempts to
learn new approaches to ministry. In America, especially, we
have such a "success" complex that we are threatened at any

thought of failure, however small. But if we examine the pages of Scripture, we can see that all the heroes of faith have had their moments of failure: Moses, Abraham, Paul, Peter, David—practically any one you can name. But the Lord used their failures to teach pointed lessons about their frailty and fallibility. Out of their weakness, he showed his strength!

So, let's dare to launch out—even on an experimental basis—and let the Lord demonstrate his ability to steer us on his course of action. He's not threatened by our failures; why should we be?

Frustration Factors

When we free ourselves for his kind of action, there will be plenty of things to try our patience and frustrate us:

•*Waiting for people to catch up with us.* We catch on to what God wants and proceed impatiently, not recognizing that it may take months, or even years, of patient teaching and encouraging until we can all move together in unity of spirit.

•*Trying to "buck city hall."* The management or hierarchy, or even the pastor, may not have a clear vision of the church as we see it, so that they throw all kinds of roadblocks to impede our progress.

•*Teaching and training leadership.* This is a slow business. It may take years to implant some of the "radical" thinking inherent in Christian truth. In the meantime, are we to bend to human opinion at the cost of surrendering solid Christian principles?

•*There's nobody more difficult than people.* And yet there's nothing more important to God, if we believe the evidence of the cross. Did you ever notice God's appeal for "forbearance"? This means putting up with the way people are and loving them anyway, always remembering that we're of the same breed and that all of us are "under construction."

A list like this could go on and on, but that would belabor the point. The important thing is to count on the great Lord of the church to be at work in his people—in me and in you—to bring us all out on top. He said it: "I will build my church."

EVERYMAN MATURE...

CHAPTER NINE

SPIRITUAL BOOT CAMPS

Every local church really should be sort of a spiritual "boot camp" where Christians can get their basic training, where they can be equipped and maintained in a state of combat readiness for the spiritual battles of life.

"Always being led in triumph in Christ" (2 Cor. 2:14) are words which validate the use of this figure, for here Christ is pictured for us as the conquering general in triumphal parade with his army. He has won the battle, and we who are his share in his victory. But though the enemy has been defeated, he still fights a last-ditch, harassing guerilla action until the day of final consummation of the war (see Col. 2:13–15). Thus—spiritual boot camps are needed.

Let's change the figure: every church should be a seminary, in the original sense of that word—a place where seeds are planted. This means that our occupation and preoccupation ought to be Christian education! Encouragingly, the recent trend toward evening schools for Christian training, seminars and conferences, adult electives in Sunday schools, is evidence that we are getting serious about our Christian education efforts.

But perhaps the greatest need is, somehow, to get Christian education back in the home, in the family scene, with the father assuming his spiritual leadership role. Discovering how to do this with vital effectiveness is difficult, but the Lord has a way, I'm sure. Here too we must seek from him that wisdom needed to understand and pursue his plan of action.

Every Man Mature

If we were to choose a theme verse to express God's aim for our training efforts it would be ". . . that we may present every man mature in Christ" (Col. 1:28).

The Apostle Paul was so concerned about this task that he adds: "For this I toil, striving with all the energy which he mightily inspires within me" (Col. 1:29).

Note the terms *toil, striving, energy*. All of these mean work, energy output on our part, so we'd better be serious, highly motivated, and fully engaged in the task. It will take all we can give it.

But note, too, where the energy comes from: "the energy which *he* mightily inspires within me." And who is *he?* From the text, the antecedent of this pronoun is *Christ*. He provides the power.

A more literal rendering of this passage says it this way:

. . . God desires to make known the riches of the glory of this revealed secret, among the nations, which is: *Christ in you*, the confident expectation (of the fulfillment) of that glory! *Him* we proclaim, encouraging and warning every man and teaching every man in all wisdom in order that we may present every man mature in Christ (fulfilling all that Christ designs to accomplish in his life). For this I also (as well as you) work hard, agonizing, according to the operation of his energizing in me with power (Col. 1:27–92).

On the one hand, this is no lazy man's course; but on the other, neither is it the unaided independent activity of the flesh. We are called to be cooperators in God's master plan, energy cells constantly being empowered from an *outside* source operating *inside* us.

Some program! *Christ in you,* the hope of glory. Hope here pictures a present experience as well as a future expectation.

Our charter is clear: every man mature. Our method is prescribed: him we proclaim. We proclaim Christ, with all the adequacy of his resources.

Proliferation

Obviously God's program is so great that we must get it spread around. We must not be so provincial in our thinking and so preoccupied with our own local situation that we have no time or thought for needs outside our own little circle. The Body of Christ is bigger than that and our concern should be for all God's people. Narrow, rigid sectarian lines of thought and action have always been condemned by God. Just check out how many words in God's description of the works of the flesh deal with this problem: *enmity, strife, jealousy, selfishness, party spirit, envy* (Gal. 5:19–21).

There is no way we can proudly parade our sectarian "distinctives" and be in accord with God's desire. God's distinctives belong to everybody.

God asks that we share the wealth of "the riches of his glory" with anyone and everyone who wants a share. So let's have no artificial boundaries! The great Head of the church wants every member to share in the bounty of the whole body.

In practical terms this means we help others to strengthen their local situation; we try to foster new assemblies of believers; we provide every positive input we can, not to build a superdenomination, but to build up the body of Christ in cooperation with the one who said, *"I will build my church."*

Putting It All Together

Putting it all together is the Lord's problem, and I don't know how he's going to do it. But I'm going to be tremendously interested in finding out!

Meanwhile I *can* cooperate quite clearly and simply by:
•Letting Christ be Lord in me.
•Listening attentively to what the Spirit says to the church.
•Praying dependently about all that concerns the fulfillment of his program for his people.
•Responding obediently to him as the expression of my love.

As history brings us ever closer to the final wrap-up, I'm increasingly concerned to make whatever personal contribution the Lord has in mind for me:

For God has allowed us to know the secret of his plan, and it is this: he purposes in his sovereign will that all human history shall be consummated in Christ, that everything that exists in Heaven or earth shall find its perfection and fulfillment in him. And here is the staggering thing . . . that in all which will one day belong to him we have been promised a share . . . so that we, as the first to put our confidence in Christ, may bring praise to his glory! (Eph. 1:9–12, Phillips)

The apostle goes on, "And you too trusted in him when you heard the message of truth."

It's clear—the Lord wants *all* of us fully engaged in the fulfilling of his plan.

CHAPTER TEN

LETTERS TO THE
TWENTIETH CENTURY
CHURCH

What would the Lord of the church write if he were to send letters to twentieth century churches? Perhaps it would go something like this:

I am the one who began the church and will have the last word on the subject. Don't you think it's time to hear what I have to say about the church? Let me ask you some important questions and point up some needed changes.

TO THE ELDERS OF THE CHURCH AT BIBLE CITY:

Why do you pride yourself on "holding to the line" on a few negative issues instead of living out the great positive values of life in me? I am God's great "Yes" and "That's true." [1] I am the great liberator, not prohibiter.

And do you not bear my name, as Christ's men and women? Why, then, do you attach yourselves to mere men and systems? Did Calvin die for you, or Luther rise again for you? Is your theology higher than my Word? [2] Did I ever ask you to fight and squabble among yourselves over my Word? Instead, I commanded you to love one another, [3] despite differences of understanding and opinion.

Oh, I know, your intentions are good, but in the meantime I'd like to have the free use of my Body. Won't you let me? Please stop saying, "But we've always done it that way!" Are your traditions more important than letting me be Lord? I may have a better way. Did you ever think to ask me? [4]

*Jesus Christ,
the Faithful Witness*

---

[1] "For the Son of God, Jesus Christ, whom we preached among you . . . was not Yes and No; but in him it is always Yes. For all the promises of God find their Yes in him. That is why we utter the Amen through him to the glory of God" (2 Cor. 1:19–20).

[2] "For the foolishness of God is wiser than men, and the weakness of God is stronger than men" (1 Cor. 1:25). "Why do you call me 'Lord, Lord,' and not do what I tell you?" (Luke 6:46).

[3] "A new commandment I give to you, that you love one another; even as I have loved you, that you also love one another" (John 13:34–35).

[4] "If any of you lacks wisdom, let him ask God, who gives to all men generously and without reproaching, and it will be given him" (James 1:5).

AND TO DIOTREPHES,[5] PASTOR OF THE CHURCH OF SELFLOVE:

Do you really think I would rest the success of my church on a few dominant personalities like you? Have you not read my Word about humility and "esteeming others better than yourself"?[6] Have you not heard that the Body, though one, has many members?[7] You seem to want to make it all mouth. But I say "the Head cannot say to the foot, I have no need of you."[8] Do you remember who the Head is?

Repent, therefore, and go back to your original assignment: "Pastor-teachers are given to equip the saints for the work of the ministry!"[9] How I groan at the way you have tied me up because you want to be the whole show while gifted men and women play spectators.

Look! I'm coming soon to evaluate your works! I'd like for you to be able to look me straight in the eye and hear my "Well done!"—not to see you hang your head in shame.[10]

Jesus Christ,
the Lamb Who Was Slain

---

[5] "I have written something to the church; but Diotrephes, who likes to put himself first, does not acknowledge my authority" (3 John 9).

[6] "Do nothing from selfishness or conceit, but in humility count others better than yourselves" (Phil. 2:3).

[7] "For just as the body is one and has many members, and all the members of the body, though many, are one body, so it is with Christ" (1 Cor. 12:12).

[8] "The eye cannot say to the hand, 'I have no need of you,' nor again the head to the feet, 'I have no need of you'" (1 Cor. 12:21).

[9] "And his gifts were that some should be . . . pastors and teachers for the equipment of the saints for a work of ministry . . ." (Eph. 4:11–12).

[10] "And now, little children, abide in him, so that when he appears we may have confidence and not shrink from him in shame at his coming" (1 John 2:28).

108

TO THE FIRST BATTLEGROUND CHURCH OF CHRIST:

Of Christ, you say? There will come a day when I shall do battle,[11] but now is not the time. Who asked you to start the fight? I could have fought instead of dying—and this is still the day for dying! [12]

Do you remember what it was that won your heart? Was it not the appeal of love? [13] I have no greater power, and neither do you. So won't you use my love and my power? How many lonely, longing hearts have you turned away? Oh, I know, you've won a few; I read the statistics in your year-end reports. But how many have you turned away?

Jesus Christ,
the Almighty

---

[11] "From his mouth issues a sharp sword with which to smite the nations, and he will rule them with a rod of iron; he will tread the wine press of the fury of the wrath of God the Almighty" (Rev. 19:15).

[12] "Always carrying in the body the death of Jesus, so that the life of Jesus may also be manifested in our bodies. For while we live we are always being given up to death for Jesus' sake, so that the life of Jesus may be manifested in our mortal flesh" (2 Cor. 4:10–11).

[13] "In this is love, not that we loved God but that he loved us and sent his Son to be the expiation for our sins" (1 John 4:10).

TO THE DEADLY ORTHODOX CHURCH OF GOD IN CHRIST:

Have you never heard, "I have come that you might have LIFE more abundant?" [14] and, "Obedience is better than sacrifice"? [15] How you weary me with your endless rounds of rituals and dogmas, all paraded in my name, while you live lives of shallowness and sham.

Don't you know that my name is used as a common curse word among the children of this world because of you? [16] Why should they think I am someone special when you don't? They see you play your "churchy" games, fight your petty squabbles, use your worldly methods, all while you disdain my resources and fail to believe my Word. [17] What else could they think? They could only say, "Who needs this dead Christ and his cross? I want to LIVE!" And all the time I long to give them life. [18]

Do you really know what it is to live? Go back to my Word. It tells you how. They must see Me, alive in you. [19]

Jesus Christ, the Firstborn from the Dead

---

[14] " . . . I came that they may have life, and have it abundantly. I am the good shepherd. The good shepherd lays down his life for the sheep" (John 10:10–11).

[15] " . . . Has the Lord as great delight in burnt offerings and sacrifices, as in obeying the voice of the Lord? Behold, to obey is better than sacrifice, and to hearken than the fat of rams" (1 Sam. 15:22).

[16] "You who boast in the law, do you dishonor God by breaking the law? For, as it is written, 'The name of God is blasphemed among the Gentiles (nations) because of you'" (Rom. 2:23–24).

[17] "But if you bite and devour one another take heed that you are not consumed by one another" (Gal. 5:15). "Are you so foolish? Having begun with the Spirit, are you now ending with the flesh?" (Gal. 3:3).

[18] "Jesus said to her, 'I am the resurrection and the life; he who believes in me, though he die, yet shall he live, and whoever lives and believes in me shall never die'" (John 11:25–26).

[19] "But we have this treasure in earthen vessels, to show that the transcendent power belongs to God and not to us" (2 Cor. 4:7).

110

TO THE FIRST RIGHT WING CHURCH:

What is my gospel? Is it meant for political liberals as well as conservatives? Democrats and Republicans alike? Can it change a hippie's heart? Can it break a heroin habit? Or is it meant just to maintain the status quo of comfortable American complacency? Have you not read, "My kingdom is not of this world—if it were my servants would fight"? [20] If political action were all I had in mind it would have been accomplished by "twelve legions of angels." [21] Instead I chose the Cross. Are you stronger than twelve legions of angels? And wiser than I?

How many hours have you squandered on pointless political intrigue? Have you told my Good News to anyone? Are you so foolish as to think you can change governments without changing men's hearts? You can still change your mind and do it my way! Ask me, I'll enable you.

Jesus Christ,
the Ruler of Kings

---

[20] "Jesus answered, 'My kingship is not of this world; if my kingship were of this world, my servants would fight, that I might not be handed over to the Jews; but my kingship is not from the world'" (John 18:36).
[21] "Do you think that I cannot appeal to my Father, and he will at once send me more than twelve legions of angels?" (Matt. 26:53).

111

TO THE CHURCH OF GLOSSOLALIA:

My heart hurts for you. I know your hunger for fulfillment and your frustration from not being fed from my Word, but do you really think you can gain spiritual ends through emotional means? Stop and think! Is speaking in tongues even mentioned as part of the fruit of the Spirit? [22] Is it listed in the qualifications for elders, as a mark of spiritual maturity? Does it accomplish my purpose for spiritual gifts so as to edify my Body? Don't you realize the true spiritual gift was given to show my people Israel their day of privilege was over and the church age begun? And that this purpose was fulfilled? [23]

The tongue is a most unruly member.[24] Why then would I give it the prominence you have assigned it? Is there so little fulfillment in the spiritual qualities of my life in you that you must seek another way? Seek rather to speak for me in clear, understandable words,[25] motivated by loving concern for others' needs, not just to express your own emotional cries understood only by

---

[22] "But the fruit of the Spirit is love, joy, peace, patience, kindness, goodness, faithfulness, gentleness, self-control; against such there is no law" (Gal. 5:22–23).

[23] "Nay, but by men of strange lips and with an alien tongue the Lord will speak to this people" (Isa. 28:11). "In the law it is written, 'By men of strange tongues and by the lips of foreigners will I speak to this people, and even then they will not listen to me, says the Lord.' Thus, tongues are a sign not for believers but for unbelievers, while prophecy is not for unbelievers but for believers" (1 Cor. 14:21–22).

[24] "So the tongue is a little member and boasts of great things. How great a forest is set ablaze by a small fire! And the tongue is a fire. The tongue is an unrighteous world among our members, staining the whole body, setting on fire the cycle of nature, and set on fire by hell. No human being can tame the tongue—a restless evil, full of deadly poison" (James 3:5–8).

[25] ". . . In church I would rather speak five words with my mind, in order to instruct others, than ten thousand words in a tongue" (1 Cor. 14:19).

me! Your intentions may be innocent enough, but the result is distortion and confusion. Change your mind, therefore, and let me show you a better way.[26]

Jesus Christ, Who Was, Who Is, Who Is to Come

---

[26] "But earnestly desire the higher gifts. And I will show you a still more excellent way. If I speak in the tongues of men and angels, but have not love, I am a noisy gong or a clanging cymbal. And if I have prophetic powers, and understand all mysteries and all knowledge, and if I have all faith, so as to remove mountains, but have not love, I am nothing" (1 Cor. 12:31–13:2).

TO THE CHURCH OF BROTHERLY LOVE— WORLDWIDE:

At last, the place of my rest![27] How good to settle down and be at home in your hearts.[28] How great to find expression for my life and my love through your yielded lives! Oh, I know you're full of flaws, and you still give me lots of problems. But at least you give me room to be who I am, to do my work in you. You pastors and teachers—I'm grateful you are being my voice, letting me speak through you amid all the conflicting claims of men who say, "Hear this! Listen to me. I have the truth!"

In the face of all the pressures and pulls of man's philosophies you heeded my Word and proclaimed my truth to a battered and bewildered world![29] And you set my people free to find their gifts and fulfill their ministries.[30] How good to have the use of my Body instead of being tied up in knots.

Well done, you elders, You who have ruled well are counted worthy of double honor.[31] The leadership of love is what I've always longed for in the church, for this is the way I lead.

---

[27] "Thus says the Lord: 'Heaven is my throne and the earth is my footstool; what is the house which you would build for me, and what is the place of my rest? All these things my hand has made and so all these things are mine, says the Lord. But this is the man to whom I will look, he that is humble and contrite in spirit, and trembles at my word' " (Isa. 66:1–2).

[28] ". . . that Christ may actually live in your hearts by faith. And I pray that you, firmly fixed in love yourselves, may be able to grasp (with all Christians) how wide and deep and long and high is the love of Christ—and to know for yourselves that love so far beyond our comprehension. May you be filled through all your being with God himself!" (Eph. 3:17–19).

[29] " 'I know your works. Behold, I have set before you an open door, which no one is able to shut; I know that you have but little power, and yet you have kept my word and have not denied my name' " (Rev. 3:8).

[30] "Now there are varieties of gifts, but the same Spirit; and there are varieties of service, but the same Lord; and there are varieties of working, but it is the same God who inspires them all in every one. To each is given the manifestation of the Spirit for the common good" (1 Cor. 12:4–7, Phillips).

[31] "Let the elders who rule well be considered worthy of double honor, especially those who labor in preaching and teaching" (1 Tim. 5:17).

And all you saints who have learned to love and be loved:[32] what a joy you are to my heart. You are my beloved Bride, and ours is the love story that will be told for eternity.[33] Keep the Word of my grace and go on to maturity. Don't marvel that the Enemy fights you and his world system hates you. That opposition is directed at me through you.[34] And I have already won the battle![35]

And don't forget—it won't be long before I see you face to face. That will be a great day for you—and for me.[36]

Jesus Christ, the Alpha and Omega, the First and Last

---

[32] "In this is love, not that we loved God but that he loved us and sent his Son to be the expiation for our sins" (1 John 4:10). "We love, because he first loved us" (1 John 4:19).

[33] "I feel a divine jealousy for you, for I betrothed you to Christ to present you as a pure bride to her one husband" (2 Cor. 11:2).

[34] "If the world hates you, know that it has hated me before it hated you. If you were of the world, the world would love its own; but because you are not of the world, but I chose you out of the world, therefore the world hates you" (John 15:18–19).

[35] "But thanks be to God, who in Christ always leads us in triumph and through us spreads the fragrance of the knowledge of him everywhere" (2 Cor. 2:14).

[36] "He who testifies to these things says, 'Surely I am coming soon.' Amen. Come, Lord Jesus!" (Rev. 22:20).

A FINAL WORD . . . TO ALL THE SAINTS:

"I will build my church . . . !"
I have said that's what I would do, and I'm doing it! Now the question is: What are you doing?"

Do you recall my words? Let me remind you once again: All authority in heaven and on earth has been given to me.[37] *That means I have all there is. Does that sound like enough? But if that's all I said you might just be afraid of me. I said also:* Look! I'm with you . . . all the way.[37] *So what more do you need?*

One more reminder: I will never, never desert you or leave you in the lurch. No, not ever! [38] *Could I put it any stronger?*

"He who has an ear, let him hear what the Spirit says to the churches."—Revelation 2:29

Jesus Christ,
King of Kings and Lord of Lords

THE END

. . . or is it the beginning?

---

[37] Matt. 28:19–20 in modern idiom.
[38] Heb. 13:5–6 paraphrased.

INDEX TO APPENDIX

MAKING DISCIPLES
By Dave Roper

1. Select key men from the larger Christian body to which you are ministering (congregation, Sunday school class, Bible study group, etc.) Note these verses for the basis of your choice: 2 Tim. 2:2; Luke 6:12, 13; Mark 3:13.
2. Begin to spend time with this select group (John 3:22). Spend leisure time with them (Mark 6:31). Get them into your home and family life; involve them in your personal life and ministry (Mark 5:37).
3. Provide additional opportunities for teaching through Bible study and discussion, reading, Scripture memorization, tapes, etc.
4. Expose them to other teachers and leaders. It takes all the saints to know all the dimensions of the knowledge of God.
5. Encourage them to open up and share their lives with one another. Set the pace by your own openness and honesty.
6. Be sensitive to teachable moments (Mark 10:13–16).
7. Don't be afraid to be hard on these men; God's men will bounce (Mark 8:18, 33; 9:1–8; 9:19).
8. Welcome adversity in their lives; these times are opportunities for advancement (Mark 4:35–41).
9. Encourage them into ministries on their own. Give them plenty of rope. You can trust the Holy Spirit in their lives. Provide counsel and encouragement. Evaluate periodically (Mark 6:7–13, 30). Move them out into positions with increasing responsibility. Gently push them out into situations beyond their depth so they have to trust the Lord.
10. Impart your vision to encourage them to disciple others and send them out (John 20:21).
11. Maintain a support base even when they are on their own. Provide help as they need it. Pray for them, write, be available for counsel.

Appendix B

SAINTS ALIVE!

I. GOD'S MASTER PLAN FOR THE CHURCH—YOU!
A study in 1 Corinthians, Chapter 12

A. **THINGS OF THE SPIRIT**—What the Spirit is doing v.1
1. UNITY OF CONFESSION—Jesus is Lord! vv.2–3
2. DIVERSITY OF FUNCTION through DEITY vv. 4–6
IN ACTION
   a. Variety of gifts (divinely given capacity for service) *from the Spirit*
   b. Variety of ministries (divinely appointed tasks or area of the exercise of a gift) *from the Lord*
   c. Variety of energizings (divinely determined results—the thing accomplished) *from God*
3. HARMONY OF COORDINATION through vv.7–11
SOVEREIGNTY OF DISTRIBUTION
Each one fulfilling his place, allowing Christ to express his life through his body
4. UNIVERSAL ILLUSTRATION—the human body vv.12–26
   a. Sharing one life in one body vv.12–13
     1. No disparagement (all needed) vv.14–17
     2. No dispute (God's arrangement) v.18
     3. No disdain (the less presentable are more indispensable) vv.19–24a
     4. No discord (all share same concerns) vv.24b–26
5. CERTAINTY OF APPLICATION
It's a fact. Now, how do we fit the facts? vv.27–31

B. Note the SETTING—between **JESUS IS LORD!** (1 Cor. 12:23)

        and **THE WAY IS LOVE!** (1 Cor. 13)

120

II. NO UNEMPLOYED SAINTS—THE HEART OF GOD'S PLAN

Discover your gifts and use them

•Do you have one? Or more? •What is their purpose?
•What are the gifts?   •How are they to be employed?
•How do I discover my gifts?

A. **Do I have one?** Read 1 Corinthians 12:1 and 4 to 7; Ephesians 4:7–8. The answer is here: "God inspires them all in *every one*"; and "to *each* is given"; and in Ephesians 4, "Grace was given to *each* of us . . . he gave gifts to men." Every Christian has a gift—maybe more than one!

B. **What are the gifts?**
   1. To define—spiritual gifts are: a special enabling for ministry; a capacity for spiritual service; or a specific function appointed by God to accomplish his purposes in the church and the world. Gifts are over and above the general capacities given to all the members of the body. For example, all are to be witnesses, but some are especially given to the church to encourage and train the others, as evangelists. All are apostles in the general sense of John 17:18, but some are specially given the ability to plant new works and pioneer in new fields of endeavor.

   Native abilities which we call "talents" are not the same as gifts. For example, a man can be an able speaker and not even be a Christian. *Gifts are divine enablings given by the Lord to accomplish the spiritual ends he desires.* The Lord will use the native abilities he has implanted (such as the natural ability to speak well or to think clearly) and will empower these as to give insight beyond the native abilities to think and expression of truth with impact beyond the normal power of speech.

   2. Gifts are of three kinds: general support gifts, sign gifts, and specific working gifts.

a. General support gifts (Eph. 4:11–16)
   (1) Apostles—men gifted to lay foundations, to build the basic support structure upon which the rest would be built. An example of the work of the apostles is the New Testament, the foundation for faith.
   (2) Prophets—God's special spokesmen to his people. Their words carry God's authority and have power to build by stimulating and encouraging. Often this gift reflects special insight into the truth and calls men back to the obedience of faith, e.g., A. W. Tozer.
   (3) Evangelists—good-news tellers; those who are able to compel a hearing of the great redeeming story of Jesus Christ to non-Christians with convicting power, e.g., Billy Graham.
   (4) Pastor-teachers—shepherds of God's flock, caring for the sheep, feeding, guiding, protecting, keeping fit and healthy. "Pastor" describes the job—shepherding. "Teacher" describes the means by which he fulfills his assignment—feeding the flock on the Word of God.

b. Sign gifts
   (1) Miracle working
   (2) Healings
   (3) Tongues
   (4) Interpretation of tongues

   The first two were the signs of the authority of the early disciples, arresting the attention of the populace, identifying with the work of Christ and attesting to their origin in the power of God. These were the credentials the apostles presented to an unbelieving world. The last two were signs to Israel that God was removing the Jews from the privileged place and turning to the Gentiles. (See 1 Cor. 14:21–22 and Isaiah 28:11.) All these seem to have served God's purpose and apparently have been set aside in the sovereign will of the Spirit of God, at least as far as we can see. If the Spirit of God should choose to use them again, we would expect it to be in line with their "sign" character.

c. Specific working gifts (Read 1 Cor. 12:8-10 and 28; Rom. 12:6-8)

 (1) Wisdom—direct insight into truth; the ability to understand how truth applies to specific situations; putting the truth to work (1 Cor. 12:8).

 (2) Knowledge—ability to investigate and systemize facts; to put them into manageable order; to recognize and relate facets of truth (1 Cor. 12:8).

 (3) Faith—better called the gift of vision, the ability to see what God wants done and the courage and faith to tackle a seemingly impossible job and accomplish it, e.g., Cameron Townsend (1 Cor. 12:9).

 (4) Prophecy—the ability to speak to men for God for their upbuilding and encouragement and consolation (1 Cor. 14:3). Also, to speak toward the unbelieving world so as to convict, open up and bring to the worship of God (1 Cor. 14:24-25).

 (5) Discernment—the ability to distinguish between the spirit of truth and the spirit of error; to spot subtle forms of phoniness and deception, e.g., Peter with Ananias and Sapphira in Acts 5 (1 Cor. 12:10).

 (6) Helps (or showing mercy)—lending a hand whenever a need appears. There are 1,001 ways to exercise this gift. "Helps" in the New Testament Greek has the sense of "holding against so as to support." Showing mercy is being moved by pity to give aid. Thus, one

describes the motivation, the other the purpose for the exercise of this gift.

(7) Teaching—giving instruction with the result
that someone is learning the truth of God
(Rom. 12:7 and 1 Cor. 12:28).

(8) Administrative gifts—keeping things in order
through organization, planning and executing
the plan.

    (a) Administration—*diakonia* (Rom. 12:7)
Household chores—caring for the multitude of detail tasks around God's household.

    (b) Leading—*proistēmi* (Rom. 12:8)
Standing before in a leadership responsibility, e.g. chairing committees, leading
meetings, etc.

    (c) Governings—*kubernēsis* (1 Cor. 12:28)
Guiding or steering the affairs of the local
church, e.g., serving as elder or overseer on
a governing board.

(9) Giving—specially called to be spiritually sensitive to needs and to make money or other
assets available for God's use (Rom. 12:8)

(10) Exhortation—the ability to call to action and
get people moving; to speak so as to motivate
or encourage (Rom. 12:8)

C. How do I discover my gifts?

In seeking to determine your spiritual gifts, follow through
the parallel to the human body as shown in the chart on
the next page:

In the HUMAN BODY, how does a member of the body (e.g., a hand) know its place of usefulness?	In the BODY OF CHRIST, how do I determine my spiritual gifts?
1. It receives orders from the head.	1. Ask the Lord, "What is my place and function in the body?" Christ as head is able and responsible to answer.
2. It has inherent features that equip it for certain functions.	2. Examine inherent features, e.g., teaching—do I enjoy studying the Word?
3. It grasps existing opportunities.	3. What is obviously at hand that I am in a position to do?
4. It sees successful results. It is productive toward designed ends.	4. Do I see that God is doing something worthwhile through me?
5. It recognizes interdependence with other members of the body.	5. How do I fit in with the other members? e.g., do I find cooperative endeavor in governing ministry?
6. It supplies a need that must be met.	6. What are current needs that need to be met? e.g., music, visitation.
7. It makes progress in proficiency.	7. Do I function better with practice? I should.
8. It experiences the gratification of usefulness.	8. Do I enjoy a sense of being used as I minister?
9. It is acknowledged by the rest of the body.	9. Do others in the body recognize and appreciate my contribution to the whole?

Then approach as you did the problem of discovering talents. Try it!

D. **What is their purpose?**
It is to build the body of Christ—his church (Eph. 4:12–16).

Christ said, "*I will build my church*—and the councils of hell shall not prevail against it" (Matt. 16). That's what he's doing—now. What are you doing?

"To each is given the manifestation of the Spirit *for the common good*" (1 Cor. 12:7).

"Let *all* things be done for edification. . . . so that all may learn and all be encouraged" (1 Cor. 14:26 and 31).

E. **How are they to be employed?** (How do I exercise my gifts?)
  1. In love. (1 Corinthians 13 is in the middle of the passage on gifts.)

     "If I speak in the tongues of men and of angels, but have not love, I am a noisy gong or a clanging cymbal. And if I have prophetic powers, and understand all mysteries and all knowledge, and if I have all faith, so as to remove mountains, but have not love, I am nothing. If I give away all I have, and if I deliver my body to be burned, but have not love, I gain nothing" (1 Cor. 13:1–3).

  2. As expressing the life of my indwelling Lord.

     "But we have this treasure in earthen vessels, to show that the transcendent power belongs to God and not to us" (2 Cor. 4:7).

     "That Christ may settle down and be at home in your hearts by your faith—that you may grasp, with all Christians, how wide and deep and long and high is the love of Christ" (Eph. 3:17–19).

  3. Remembering that they are gifts given by his sovereign authority (1 Cor. 12:11 and 18). There is no ground for pride.

     As we do these things, our Lord will be seen to be at work in us as members of his body expressing his life (1 Cor. 12:27).

To discover your gifts and employ them is the most exciting discovery possible. It is to recognize the purpose for which God intended you!

> And he himself gave the apostles, the prophets,
>   the evangelists, the pastor-teachers,
> toward the fitting out of the saints for a work
>   of ministry, for the building of the body of Christ—
> until we all arrive at the oneness of the faith and
>   of the full knowledge of the Son of God, to a mature
> man, to the measure of the stature of the fullness of
>   Christ—that we may no longer be babies, being
> tossed back and forth—but maintaining truth in
>   love, we may grow up in every way into Christ, the
> head. For it is from the head that the whole body is
>   a harmonious structure, knit together by the
> joints with which it is provided, and grows by the
>   proper functioning of individual parts to its full
> maturity in love.

Ephesians 4:11–16
(a literal rendering)

APPENDIX C

PRINCIPLES OF THE MINISTRY
Compiled by David Roper

1. Establish and maintain the proper priorities (Phil. 1:1-9).
   A ministry is analogous to building a tower. It rests on a series
   of underlying foundations. If the foundations are weak then
   the whole structure will totter. If we weaken at any level, we
   must stop building above until that level is strengthened.

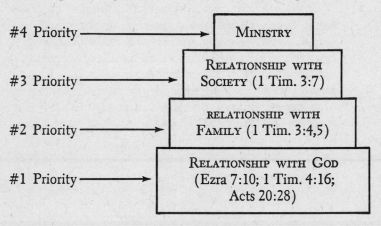

#4 Priority ⟶ MINISTRY

#3 Priority ⟶ RELATIONSHIP WITH SOCIETY (1 Tim. 3:7)

#2 Priority ⟶ RELATIONSHIP WITH FAMILY (1 Tim. 3:4,5)

#1 Priority ⟶ RELATIONSHIP WITH GOD (Ezra 7:10; 1 Tim. 4:16; Acts 20:28)

2. Our authority as leaders is derived from our obedience to the
   truth (1 Tim. 4:12; John 10:37; Heb. 13:17; Judges 6).
3. The basis of any ministry is faith. It is "by faith" that God's
   work is accomplished (Heb. 11). It is not by planning, by
   organization or by self-effort. While these have their place, we
   must be flexible and easily led by the Holy Spirit. The direction of our ministry and the speed with which that ministry
   grows is the prerogative of the Holy Spirit alone (John 6:28,
   29; 2 Cor. 3:4-6; Col. 1:29).
4. The strongest ministries are *team* ministries. Since God's way
   is to operate through a body, rather than venture into a ministry alone we must let God develop a team relationship first
   (Deut. 32:30; Matt. 18:19-20; John 1:35-51). Note that

Jesus spent an entire year with four to six men before he began his public ministry.

5. Life-related biblical instruction must underlie all our efforts to bring men to maturity. Teach the Scriptures methodically and expositorily. Teach the "whole counsel of God." Teach repetitively the great liberating principles of Scripture (2 Tim. 3:14–4:2; Acts 20:17–32; John 21:15–17; 2 Cor. 4:1–6; Eph. 4:15–16).

6. The goal of our ministry is to "present every man *mature in Christ*" (Col. 1:28). Every activity must be evaluated in the light of that goal.

7. As we teach, we must look for "faithful men who can teach others" and invest the bulk of our time in the lives of these men. The Lord established the pattern in his ministry. He taught the crowds, but his training ministry was concentrated in the Twelve. Note John 17:6, 9, 17.

8. We are a body! (1 Cor. 12; Rom. 12:3–8). Therefore we need to recognize the distinctiveness of that body.

Distinctives

   a. Every member has a unique function. He cannot depreciate his place in the body.
   b. No member carries on all the functions of the body.
   c. The members of a body are interdependent.

Implications

   a. We need one another! The best ministries are team ministries composed of men who possess varying gifts.
   b. It is wrong to insist that anyone follow one man alone. Men need an exposure to many members of the body.
   c. One major thrust of our ministry must be to help others find and develop their spiritual gifts and exercise them with all their heart in their appointed place.

9. The key to effective evangelism is to get the body to function correctly (John 17:20–21; Eph. 4:16; John 13:34, 35).

10. Gifted men are given to the body to equip the saints to do the work of the ministry (Eph. 4:11–16). Spiritual leaders in

any group are like player-coaches who have as their primary aim the training and engagement in the ministry of individual believers.

11. The leadership shortage is always with us. When we look for leaders, let's start where the Lord did. (See Matt. 9:37–38.)

12. The Body of Christ is not a hierarchy. We have only one Lord, and all others are brothers (Matt. 23). Note these verses for characteristics of a spiritual leader: Heb. 13:7, 17; 1 Thess. 2:1–20; Acts 20:17–38.

13. Magnify the ministry of others. Are we as excited about others' ministry as about our own?

14. Leadership is not lordship but servanthood. The measure of our spiritual leadership is not how many we rule over, but rather how many we serve (Mark 9:33–37; 10:35–45).

15. People are God's most important product. They take precedence over any program (Mark 5:21–36; Mark 6:30–37).

16. Hit men hard. God's men will bounce when the truth is spoken in love (2 Cor. 2:15–16).

17. Look for men like the Gerasene demoniac (Mark 5:1–20). This man evangelized that entire countryside. As far as we know, Jesus spent only a few hours in that region.

18. Size does not equal success. God always perpetuates faith through a remnant. Don't count noses. Operate on the basis of biblical principles and God will bring enlargement (Acts 2:47). When we feed our people, we won't need to waste time on promotional gimmicks.

19. 2 Timothy 2:24–26 is S.O.P. (standard operating procedure).

20. The harvest is at the end of the age, not the end of the meeting. Discouragement grows out of unrealistic expectations. The seed doesn't spring up immediately after it's sown. Let God bring it to maturity in his time and he will go beyond our expectations (Mark 4:26–32; 1 Cor. 3:5–9; Isa. 55:11).

NEW TESTAMENT REFERENCES
ON DEACONS

For your further study we have listed all the occurrences of *diakonos, diakonia* and *diakoneo* in the New Testament. The ones marked with an asterisk have been cited in the body of this study.

Diakonos in the New Testament:

Matthew 20:26; 22:13; 23:11
Mark 9:35; *10:43
John 2:5, 9; *12:26
Romans 13:4; 15:8; *16:1
1 Corinthians 3:5
2 Corinthians *3:6; 6:4; *11:15, *23
Galatians 2:17
Ephesians 3:7; 6:21
Philippians *1:1
Colossians 1:7, 23, *25; 4:7
1 Timothy 3:8, 12; 4:6

Diakonia in the New Testament:

Luke 10:40
Acts 1:17, 25; 6:1, *4; 11:29; 12:25; 20:24; 21:19
Romans 11:13; *12:7; *15:31
1 Corinthians 12:5; *16:15
2 Corinthians *3:7–9; 4:1; *5:18; *6:3; 8:4; 9:1, 12, 13; 11:8
Ephesians *4:12
Colossians 4:17
1 Timothy 1:12
2 Timothy *4:5, 11
Hebrews *1:14
Revelation 2:19

Diakoneo in the New Testament:

Matthew 4:11; 8:15; *20:28; *25:44; 27:55
Mark *1:13, 31; 10:45; 15:41
Luke 4:39; 8:3; 10:40 *12:37; *17:8; *22:26–27
John 12:2, 26
Acts 6:2; *19:22
Romans 15:25
2 Corinthians *3:3; *8:19–20
1 Timothy *3: 10, *13
2 Timothy *1:18
Philemon 13
Hebrews *6:10
1 Peter *1:12; 4:10–11

[Resource materials: Kittel, *Theological Dictionary of the New Testament; Englishman's Greek Concordance*]

HOW WE GOT IN THE BODY!
(The Baptism of the Holy Spirit)

If you are "in Christ," how did you get there?

1 Corinthians 12:13 tells us: "For just as the body is one and has many members, and all the members of the body, though many, are one body—so it is with Christ. *For by one Spirit we were all baptized into one body . . .*"

Analyzing this last phrase, we need to determine (1) the meaning of the word "baptize," and (2) the grammatical structure of the sentence.

(1) "Baptize" is originally a Greek word. We borrowed it and transliterated it into the English language by simply changing one letter. Therefore we cannot rely on our twentieth century understanding of this word, but must seek to discover what it meant in its Greek usage in the first century, when 1 Corinthians was written. When we do this, we discover it had two meanings:

  (a) A ceremonial usage, in which a ritual dipping symbolized something, e.g., warriors "baptized" the tips of their spears in blood before battle, symbolizing the intent to kill by letting the blood of the enemy.

  (b) A mechanical or "real" usage, where "to baptize" is *to place into or introduce into, causing a change of relationship*, e.g., a ship was "baptized" in the harbor when it sank.

In this verse it is obvious that the action described is *real*—not symbolic or ritual, so we take the second meaning, as in (b) above. When we employ this meaning in the verse, it reads: "For by one Spirit we were all *placed into* one body."

This is how we got in the body of Christ: The Spirit of God placed us into living union with him, our living Head, when we received Christ as our Lord!

(2) The verb "baptized" describes completed action at a point of time—*something that has already happened to those who are Christ's*. That's why the complete form says "we *were* baptized." Note also that this verb is a *passive* form, signifying that we were the ones receiving the action, not the ones acting. This means that *the Spirit of God did the placing into the body*. We simply *received* the gracious ministry of the Holy Spirit. *He* placed us into the body so we could enjoy the new relationship with Christ. This is the baptizing ministry of the Spirit, by which all who know Christ were taken *out of Adam* and placed "*in Christ.*"

What does that mean to me? Quite a lot—it means *I'm identified with Christ in all that he is and does:* "For as many of you as were baptized into Christ have put on Christ" (Gal. 3:27).

•I shared his death (Rom. 6:6).
•I share his resurrection life (Rom. 6:8).
•As a member of his body, I share *all* that is his (1 Cor. 3:22–23).

In Time and Eternity!
  Rom. 8:14–21
  Rom. 14:8–9

THE SPIRIT'S MINISTRIES TO US

Getting it in perspective:

•CONVICTED *by the Spirit:* we are shown our need to believe in Christ as our Lord and thus gain all the value of his death and life (John 16:7–11).
•BORN *of the Spirit:* we enter into God's family as his dearly loved children (John 3:3 & 6; Titus 3:5–7; 1 John 3:1–2).
•BAPTIZED *by the Spirit:* we are placed into the body of Christ as living members joined to our living Lord (1 Cor. 12:12–13).

•*SEALED by the Spirit:* we are made safe and secure under God's ownership. (Eph. 1:13–14).

•*INDWELT by the Spirit:* we become his temple, the place for offering the sacrifice of praise (John 14:16–17; 1 Cor. 6:19–20; Eph. 2:19–22; Heb. 13:15).

•*FILLED with the Spirit:* we are controlled and empowered for useful life and service, showing forth the fruit of the Spirit (Eph. 5:18; Gal. 5:22–23).

FOLLOW-UP SCHEDULE FOR NEW CHRISTIANS

By David Roper

The order of these topics may be changed as needed. Have in mind where these new Christians are, what their needs are, and how to apply these topics to those specific needs.

1. Nature of the transaction
   a. What is the gospel?
   b. Explanation of terms
      (1) reconciliation
      (2) justification
      (3) propitiation
      (4) redemption
2. How to maintain a love relationship
   a. Commitment (Rom. 12:1)
   b. Communication
      (1) The Word (1 Pet. 2:2, 3)
      (2) Prayer (Phil. 4:6, 7)
   c. Confidence or trust (1 Pet. 5:7)
   d. Honesty (1 John 1:9)
3. Basis of spiritual power (John 6 or Campus Crusade *Bird Book* [Filling of Spirit] "Christ in you" concept)
4. Purpose of tests (Rom. 5:1–10; James 1:1–15; 2 Cor. 4:7–12)
5. Meeting temptation: spiritual warfare (Eph. 6)
6. Sovereignty of God (Rom. 9 and Eph. 1)
7. Authority of Scriptures (1 Thess. 2:13: not so much an apologetic approach but call to obedience, God's word a revelation not to be ignored)
8. How to study the Word (simple approach)
9. Prayer
10. Witnessing
11. Spiritual gifts (1 Cor. 12)
12. Nature of the Body (Eph. 4 or 1 Cor. 12)

13. God's program for the world: survey of prophecy; purpose for Israel and church
14. Interpersonal relationships: home, business, etc. (Eph. 5:18–6:9 or Phil. 2:1–18)
15. Christian graces (Gal. 5)
16. Leadership-servanthood concept of Christian service
17. Christian view of sex (1 Cor. 6 and 1 Thess. 4)

TWELVE WAYS TO DOMINATE INSTEAD OF LEADING

1. Use your superior knowledge of Scripture to snow the opposition.
2. Wrest Scripture out of context to use as a club.
3. Intimidate by a display of temper, shouting, pouting and other such kid stuff.
4. Threaten to quit if they don't do it your way.
5. Seek support for your position by privately persuading other elders.
6. Be stubborn and hold out for your way until everyone gets tired and gives in.
7. Sneak the action through when some of the opposition is out of town.
8. Make public announcement of a decision before it's made by the board; then they will have to do it your way.
9. Cut down those who disagree with you in your messages from the pulpit.
10. Pull your rank; tell them, "The Lord told me *this* is the way we do it."
11. Think through all the answers, plan all the programs, and just tell them what we're going to do. Don't ever open the door for them to think, make suggestions or plan with you.
12. Be the whole show on the platform at every meeting. That way nobody else can get a word in. Don't ever ask your men to lead a meeting, pray, read Scripture, teach or anything like that. After all, they've never been trained and you have (beyond your intelligence).

"But the wisdom from above is first pure, then peaceable, gentle, open to reason, full of mercy and good fruits, without uncertainty or insincerity."—James 3:17

Appendix H

MARKS OF MATURITY

1. Stability and consistency (1 Pet. 1:13)
2. Walking by faith (Rom. 8:14)
3. Openness to correction (1 Pet. 5:5–6)
4. Nondefensive attitude (1 Pet. 5:5–6)
5. A teachable spirit (1 Cor. 2:6–13)
6. Honesty before God (1 John 1:5–10)
7. Love extended without reservation (John 13:34–35, Matt. 5:48)
8. Acceptance of conflict and suffering as part of the growth pattern (Rom. 5:3)
9. Freedom from fear (1 John 4:17–18)
10. Knowing good from evil in subtle distinction (Heb. 5:14)
11. Confidence (1 Tim. 3:13)
12. Knowing and exercising right priorities (John 11:9–10)
13. Willingness to surrender one's rights for Christ's sake (Phil. 2:5–9)
14. Accepting an obscure place without requiring praise to keep going (2 Cor. 4:5)
15. Faithfulness in assuming and fulfilling assignments, availability and follow-through (1 Cor. 4:2)
16. Submission to authority (Rom. 12:1–3)
17. Liberty resulting from obedience (John 8:34)

FRIENDSHIP EVANGELISM THROUGH HOME BIBLE CLASSES

In these days when so many are writing off the Christian message with hardly a look, does it follow that God is out of business and that Christians haven't a chance to reach their friends and neighbors with the "Good News" about Jesus Christ? Obviously not. God is still calling out a people for his name! There are still hungry hearts around. What we need is to discover how we can be used to get the two together. We need not be dismayed by the situation, but we should be reexamining the basis of our efforts to reach those without Christ to see if we are using the means which God has made available.

One of these means is the home Bible class, or Bible discussion group.

In Acts 10, God used the home of Cornelius, a Roman centurion, to introduce the gospel to the Gentiles. He is using this same approach today.

Here's How It Works

(1) A *right attitude* about Christian separation is basic. We must be approachable and outgoing as our Lord Jesus was to the publicans and sinners. This means that we may have to change our minds (like Peter in Acts 10) about what is "unclean." Our Lord expects from us communication without contamination. But we cannot communicate the gospel without some contact with the non-Christian world.

(2) It proceeds on the basis of a *missionary approach*. We should consider ourselves missionaries to the twentieth century pagans. We must reach them where they are, in their culture pattern, using their language.

(3) We need *unmixed motives*, desiring to give them an opportunity to consider the claims of Christ upon their hearts and lives as we present him from the Scriptures. We are not presenting

ourselves or our church; we are presenting Christ as Lord! (2 Cor. 4:5) We are to teach the authoritative Word of God without personal dogmatism, giving ample opportunity for questions and discussion—speaking the truth in love (Eph. 4:15).

(4) The genius of this approach seems to be in the fact that many folks are willing to gather in the *informal, relaxed atmosphere* of a living room to discuss the Scriptures, and thus consider the gospel message. Many will find Christ to be the very One they need!

Here Are the Basic Elements

(1) A *Christian couple* who are willing to open their home and invite their friends in for such informal studies. A newly saved couple make ideal hosts, because of their many unexplored contacts and their earnest desire to share the wealth of their new found faith with their friends and neighbors. The following "Helpful Hints for Hosts and Hostesses" offer some further guidelines:

- Try to arrange everything to produce a friendly, informal atmosphere for the class. Aim at making *nonbelievers* feel at home. Be sure to have ashtrays and matches available. Provide informal group seating.
- Avoid "churchy" expressions; be natural and casual in your attitude and actions.
- Remember people's names and introduce them around. (Keeping a guest book and studying it between classes will help you learn their names.)
- Have Bibles available for folks who don't have them.
- Have Catholic versions available, preferably the Confraternity edition. Have a good concordance available for reference.
- Observe your guests as the lesson progresses and ask questions of the teacher concerning points which appear to be bothering them.
- Serve refreshments to provide a time of fellowship, but keep it simple.

- Expect that some inquirers will stay late to ask questions. Be prepared to let them stay. Don't start turning out the lights!
- Use phone and personal calls to invite people to the class. Pray!

(2) A *committed teacher* who is willing to spend the necessary hours of study time to be able to expound the Word clearly. This man need not be a "pro," but must be a student. He should be willing to say "I don't know" when necessary, then offer to search out the answer from the Scriptures. He must rely on the authority of the Word of God and be personally convinced of its integrity and trustworthiness. Further "Tips for Teachers" are suggested as follows:

- Present a positive Christianity. *Give inquirers something to believe.* Keep away from negative attitudes as much as possible. Avoid "churchy" clichés and speech unintelligible to the non-Christian.
- Be informal; inject humor; help people to relax.
- Spend time on *how* to present the lesson as well as on *what* to present. Try novel approaches to gain interest and attention.
- Keep reading Christian literature. Stay current with the times through selected periodicals. Use illustrations that relate the Bible to life.
- Encourage discussion by the class at any time, but guide it so that it expounds the truth of the passage being considered.
- Keep flexible. Be willing to answer questions from nonbelievers at any time during the lesson, but be sure to arrive at a scriptural conclusion to the question.
- Make application of the truth to life!
- Allow the Lord to show his grace and love through you. *Speak the truth in love.*
- Point the lesson toward an open, intelligent consideration of the person and work of Jesus Christ in the gospel. Expect non-Christians to be deciding about where he fits in their life. Be sensitive to your opportunities to help them *personally* decide for him.

(3) *Cooperating Christians* who recognize the opportunity to bring the Christian message to their friends are needed to pray for

the prospects, invite them to the class, personally witness, and encourage their guests to consider the claims of Christ. Constant education is necessary to prevent classes from becoming a cozy Christian gathering with a nice clean "antiseptic" atmosphere with no life-and-death character. The *local church* is the primary place for receiving Christian instruction, and these classes cannot become a substitute for church. If they do, they lose vitality and fail to fulfill God's purpose as an *evangelistic* ministry. It seems that relatively few twentieth century Christians have grasped and used this basic New Testament method of evangelism which we see reflected in the pages of Scripture. The tendency today seems to be to bring people to church to find the Lord, whereas it seems clear that our Lord intended *an outgoing ministry of reaching people where they are.* See more under the following "Clues for Cooperating Christians":

- The primary purpose of the class is to share the "Good News" of the gospel with our friends and neighbors who have not yet trusted Christ, so invite them to attend with you.
- Be friendly and alert to the opportunity to help someone know the Lord. Remember, each of us is a walking portrayal of Christ in a life.
- Be careful not to offend by a negative approach, "downing" their religion, being critical or self-righteous.
- Let the visitors ask their questions first. If you ask one, be sure it is keyed to their interest and need.
- Don't talk about your church. *Do* talk about *your Lord.* We are not interested in proselyting for any church but the one in Ephesians 1:22–23.
- Pray for your own opportunities to witness at the class, for the teacher, for the prospects.
- During the lesson period, let the teacher do the teaching. Your opportunity to talk will come later, after the lesson time, in private conversations with the visitors.
- Be sensitive and yielded to the Spirit's direction; sympathetic to the needs of the visitors, *filled with the compassion of Christ* (2 Cor. 5:14–15).

(4) The *format we have found most usable* is to teach through a book of the Bible in an expository manner, not verse by verse, but presenting the progress of thought of the book. Romans, John's Gospel, and Hebrews seem to be the best books to use. The first eight chapters of Romans, presented in ten or twelve weeks, is a good way to start.

(5) A *time of informal sociability* after the class with the serving of refreshments is another helpful ingredient. This often results in little knots of people gathering together and discussing the lesson, or a time when the guests ask their questions of the one who brought them, and it provides a natural opportunity for a word of personal testimony.

A Final Word of Caution

This information is designed to help those who want to enter into the exciting and profitable home Bible class ministry. It reflects the observations and experience of several people over a period of years in a number of areas. However, it is by no means intended to represent all that could be said or the last word on the subject. *You* could be the one to discover more of what the Lord wants to do with this particular ministry—so keep your mind and heart open to him!

The history of the church is still being written—in terms of human lives. And *there is no substitute for allowing Christ himself to be Lord of his church. Our dependence is to be on him!*

APPENDIX J

TELCO BIBLE STUDY

FOR

All telephone people who desire to take part in an objective study of the Bible.

PURPOSE

To intelligently discuss, as a group, what a Bible passage says, what it means, and what its application is to individuals today.

PROCEDURE

1. The Bible studies are held on a "Conference Leader" basis, rotating among all men who are willing to lead a study.
2. Each person should bring his own Bible (all versions are welcome.
3. The Bible will be the basis of group standards. All questions will be answered, insofar as possible, from the Bible.
4. Denominational issues are not an appropriate subject for discussion.
5. Individual expositions are limited to three minutes.
6. Comments and discussions should be centered on the passage under study. References to other Bible passages should be avoided unless the cross reference is essential to an understanding of the passage under study.
7. The study format will be to read one chapter (or a reasonable portion thereof). Following the reading of the passage, determine through group discussion:
   a. What it says (in our own words).
   b. What it means (viewed objectively).
   c. What its application is to us personally (viewed subjectively).

APPENDIX K
SOME STICKY ISSUES

We are indebted to Ron Ritchie for most of these questions, drawn from his experience in talking to pastors and church leaders. The local references to "what we do" at our local church in no way infer that we are doing everything right, for, like everyone else, we are still being taught of God and are just learning. In citing these examples we are simply attempting to share something of what we have learned, and our experience, interpreted in the light of God's Word, is the only source we have for living examples.

Question: *If I follow and teach what this book presents, won't I be fired?*
We don't know. Your responsibility is to declare and obey the truth. You might be fired, but if so you can expect the Lord to open doors to a new ministry. As your Lord, he's responsible for your life, but you may be able to help reestablish God's order where you are. Just be sure you are responding to his direction and following his time schedule. Seek to understand the truth about these matters for yourself, then patiently and lovingly teach the truth he shows you. All the while remember how long it took you to catch on, and exercise lots of patience.

Question: *How can I change my existing board?*
You can't; only the Lord can! So don't try. But you can graciously help them to understand the truth as you see it and seek to move out *together* on the basis of your mutal understanding of God's way.

Question: *What's wrong with majority vote for board decisions?*
It avoids the necessity to trust the Lord to give a spirit of unity and reverts back to "the will of the majority" instead of finding the mind of Christ on the matter. It also encourages political pressuring and party spirit. We feel certain one of the Lord's

146

biggest heartaches is the broken fellowships caused by lack of unity. Politics are bad enough, but church politics are far worse because this kind of activity is so out of character with the concept of the Body. Have you ever noticed how often splits occur among democratically governed churches?

Questions: *How can we be sure who has the Lord's mind on a matter in a ten-against-one split on an issue? Is the one right or are the ten?*

See the illustration given on pages 36 and 37. The principle in this situation is to wait on the Lord in dependent prayer. We can also discuss issues together and seek added information that might clarify them, but all without pressuring to move things our way.

Question: *If I'm an elder, but not on the pastoral staff of the church, do I still have a pastoral role?*

You certainly do! First, you are to care for the sheep (be a pastor over the flock) which God has called you to govern. All the decisions you are called on to make are to be under the direction of the Chief Shepherd, the Lord Jesus, for the well-being of his flock. In addition you undoubtedly have, or should have, a portion of that flock toward whom you have a direct teaching, overseeing, or discipling ministry.

Question: *How do you choose elders?*

By the procedure described in chapter 2, pages 21 and 23, measuring the men God has made available against the scriptural yardstick set forth in the New Testament.

Question: *Are there grounds for dismissing elders?*

Flagrant sin with no repentance is grounds for dismissal and public exposure, as per 1 Timothy 5:17–20, but undertaken with loving firmness and redemptive motives.

Question: *Can elders ever take a leave of absence?*

Whenever there is a higher priority demand, an elder not only may but must take the necessary time aside to set his house in order. This is particularly true of crisis situations in the family, for if things are not in good shape at home, he will be too preoccupied to govern well in God's family. Either the elder himself

or his fellow elders should be free to request a leave, without
censure, but rather with a deep sense of concern to seek an early
answer to the problem, so that neither his own family or God's
family is hurting for lack of his ministry.

Question: *How do you remove an elder who is not functioning?*
First, try to encourage him, by exhortation and personal help,
to begin to function. If, after you have done all you can to help
him shape up, he still is not moving, it would seem wise to ask
him to consider his accountability to God in holding down the
position but not performing. If there is still no response, he may
then be asked to resign.

Question: *How do elders control all the activities and the
doctrinal purity in Bible classes, etc.?*
They don't. The job of superintending and controlling belongs
to the Holy Spirit—and he's not about to be replaced by you or
me! Trust the Lord to guide them just as he does you. We are
not God's police patrol. When discipline is necessary in the areas
where we have direct, personal responsibility, then we should
follow the biblical pattern of Matthew 18:15–17. But remember
—to treat someone "as a Gentile and a tax collector" is to put him
in the place of one who does not know the Lord Jesus. And how
are we to act toward those?

Question: *Do you have women elders?*
Even in these days of women's lib we should have no embarrassment or hesitancy in answering, "No—no women elders,"
but only because God has already said it: "Let a woman learn in
silence with all submissiveness. I permit no woman to teach or to
have authority over men; she is to keep silent. For Adam was
formed first, then Eve; and Adam was not deceived, *but the
woman was deceived* and became a transgressor" (1 Tim.
2:11–14).

Question: *How do you operate your membership program?*
We don't have one, because the Spirit of God is adding to the
church daily those who believe. The important thing is that he
makes each believer a member of Christ's body. We do have a
covenant of fellowship for people who want local identification

with a church, but this is for their benefit, to give a sense of belonging. However, many who enjoy our fellowship find it fully satisfying just to belong to Christ and his body, and this is fine with us. We feel free to ask some to sign the covenant if we think they need this tie, but their spiritual state and well-being are our primary concern, not their belonging to our "club."

Question: *What is the attitude of your people toward the apparently "secret" meetings of your governing board?*

As far as we can tell, their attitude is one of relief that the responsibility is ours and not theirs—except when things don't go well and needs are not being met; then they let us know where they are hurting so we can move to the rescue.

Question: *How do you keep your people informed?*

Badly, at times. But we try to be alert to communication needs and handle through the weekly bulletin, occasional news sheets, reports on board actions and finances. Pulpit announcements and occasional congregational meetings are also a help. Pages 51 and 52 for more on this.

Question: *How do you incorporate spiritual gifts?*

We are constantly evaluating ourselves and our people in the light of spiritual gifts and ministries to see where and how all the members fit into the body. One of the pastor's chief occupations is to solve the "spiritual unemployment" problems. We sometimes have a "Spiritual Gift Employment Service" available on Sundays for people to inquire about current training and ministry opportunities they may wish to check out. We are constantly teaching on this subject and trying to help Christians find their place of usefulness and fulfillment.

About Bob Smith—

The man—a combination of lively intelligence, subtle humor, keen insight into people, gentleness of spirit plus an aggressive attitude of "Let's get the job done."

The pastor—an engineer by training with thirteen years of experience in steel fabricating prior to an equal number of years as an associate pastor at Peninsula Bible Church. His impact on PBC has been greatest in expository Bible teaching to adult groups, scriptural marriage counseling, home Bible class development, and church government.

The believer—an overwhelming belief that Christ will be head of his church and head of each believer if only we allow him opportunity; a quiet unshakable confidence in Christ's power to live in and through each member of his Body. An acceptance of responsibility as an elder and pastoral spiritual leader which is based on total commitment that the ministry of the church is to be carried out by each believer.

The husband and father—a successful husband of thirty-seven years and father of twin sons. A compassionate neighbor and father figure to many youngsters and young adults who prize highly their friendship with Bob Smith.